FINDING THE WAY THROUGH JOHN

by

John Fenton
Canon of Christ Church, Oxford

MOWBRAY
LONDON & OXFORD

First published 1988
by A. R. Mowbray & Co. Ltd,
Saint Thomas House, Becket Street, Oxford, OX1 1SJ

Typeset by Acorn Bookwork, Salisbury.
Printed in Great Britain by Billing & Sons Ltd, Worcester.

British Library Cataloguing in Publication Data

Fenton, John, *1921–*
    Finding the way through John.
    1. Bible. N.T. John – Commentaries
    I. Title
    226′.507

ISBN 0-264-67142-2

To Linda with love
on the twenty-fifth anniversary
of our wedding

Contents

Preface

Many thanks are due to William Purcell and Robert Williams, of Mowbray's Publishing Division, for suggesting that I should write a book such as this, and for offering me the title; and to Bernadette O'Reilly, of the Theology Faculty Office, for typing an illegible manuscript.

I have deliberately avoided footnotes and Biblical references, in order to make for easier reading; but I am not unaware that all the ideas expressed here have come from books I have read and people to whom I have listened; and I thank them all. Some of the literature on John's gospel will be found at the end of this book, under Books on John's Gospel.

The only abbreviations that occur are as follows:

AV   *The Authorised Version of the Bible* (1611)
RV   *The Revised Version of the Bible* (Old Testament 1884, New Testament 1881)
RSV   *The Revised Standard Version of the Bible* (Old Testament 1952, New Testament 1946)
NEB   *The New English Bible* (1970)

John Fenton

Introduction

This book is about one of the four gospels, The Gospel according to John. We shall be considering it on its own and trying to understand it in isolation from the other three, almost as though they did not exist. When on occasion we do look at them, it will usually be to contrast John with them, so that we can see John's book in its individuality more clearly. This way of looking at a gospel may seem strange and need some explanation, because usually in the past people have not made distinctions between these four books; everything in them has been treated as though their authors shared the same point of view and presented the same message. The idea that evangelists are individual writers, each putting forward distinct and different presentations of the good news, has arisen fairly recently and is still unfamiliar to many people; when they hear that a passage is to be read from, say, Matthew or John they do not immediately have a mental picture or overall view of what that writer's intention was, or how he differs from the others. It may help to see the four gospels as separate and distinct books if we start from the question, how did it come about that there were four gospels, and not just one?

It has to be said straight off that we know very little for certain about the origin of the gospels; and that most, some would say all, of what we know is derived from reading them and comparing them with one another. Such information as there is about the books and their authors that comes from outside the books themselves is usually of a late date and may itself be based on the books, and not be reliable independent evidence. It is probably best to assume that we know nothing more about the gospels and their authors than what we can find through studying them. This is the only way to discover when they were written, and where, and whether they are dependent on one another in some way, and what the purpose was for which each was written. And it must be said again that there is no complete agreement among scholars on the answer to any of these questions.

A view that is widely held at the present time, and has now been maintained by some of the experts in this field for a century and a half, is that the earliest of the four gospels, the one that was written first, was Mark: it is the shortest of the four, and, until it was thought to be the earliest, it was the least popular. Matthew, it is thought, enlarged Mark, changing the order of events mainly in the first half of his book, and adding much new material; he seems to have been writing for Christians who expressed their faith in Jesus and their attitude to the Jewish law in a different way from the readers for whom Mark's book had been written. Then a third writer produced a very much larger single work in two volumes, the first of which is now known as The Gospel according to Luke, and the second as The Acts of the Apostles; he too, it is thought, made much use of Mark, but, whereas Matthew had used almost the whole of that book, Luke omitted more; he too added new material, some that was not in any other gospel, some that was already added in by Matthew; and it may be that he derived this from his knowledge of Matthew. He certainly seems to have made changes to Mark that are similar to those made by Matthew: they both add birth stories, a genealogy, the teaching of Jesus and the resurrection appearances – all topics on which Mark must have seemed to them inadequate. The dates when this was happening are not known, but a commonly held opinion is that it was during the last thirty years of the first century that Mark first, then Matthew, and then Luke, were composed and made available; they were certainly being quoted in the first half of the second century.

One of the features of these three books that surprises us is that they are almost completely anonymous. The name Mark does not appear anywhere in the text of his book, though it may have stood as a heading, The Gospel according to Mark, or simply, According to Mark; but we cannot be sure even about this. The reason why we do not know is because the earliest manuscripts of Mark (or of any other New Testament book) are no longer in existence; and his book is not quoted with the name Mark until well into the second century. The name Matthew occurs twice in his book; but if it is right to think that he is using Mark, and is totally dependent on him for the main part of his story, it becomes very difficult to see how this gospel can have been written by the man called Matthew in the book, who was one of the twelve disciples of Jesus. It seems more likely that Matthew is a pseudonym, or pen-name, rather than the name of the actual author of the book. Luke's name is not mentioned in his book, but in the second volume he uses the first person plural, we, in some of his accounts of Paul's journeys, and so could be thought to be claiming to be a companion of the apostle. The authors of these three gospels, therefore, stood back in the shadows of their books, and did not obtrude themselves into their narratives; we shall find rather more reference to the writer of the gospel in John's book, however; the author has now become a character in his own story.

There has been much discussion, both in the ancient church and in the last two centuries, about the author of John's gospel, but there are no firm conclusions that are universally held. In fact, the situation at the moment is that there is complete disagreement between opposing points of view. The position that will be adopted in this book is that the author of John was a Christian of the late first century, or very early second; and that he knew, or at least knew of, some or all of the other three gospels, but decided that what was needed was a new and very different presentation of the Christian faith. He refers to an otherwise unknown follower of Jesus as the disciple whom Jesus loved, but he never gives us his name. He is usually presented as in company with Peter, and as in some sense superior to him. It came to be thought that Mark's gospel contained the reminis-

cences of Peter, written by Mark; so it may be that the author of
John is claiming to be the disciple whom Jesus loved, one who
was in a better position to write a gospel than Mark, or his
successors Matthew and Luke. Like the other three evangelists,
he wrote a book that was meant to stand on its own, without the
support or corroboration of other gospels; he intended his book
to provide the way to faith in Jesus, and thus to be the means by
which his readers could receive God's supreme and final gift of
eternal life. He never used the name John in his book to refer to
himself; when he did use it, it was always in reference to John the
Baptist. But we shall follow the convention of using the name
John, and we shall mean by it nothing more than the author of
the book that is commonly known as The Gospel according to
John, whoever he was, or the book itself.

Much of this must seem strange to a present-day reader, who
may not have come across some of the literature on this subject
that has been produced in the last fifty to a hundred years: here
we have books that claim to be by people who did not write
them; authors who quote another author extensively but without any acknowledgement; a writer who puts himself into his
account of events at which he was not in fact present and devises
for himself an extraordinary title, the disciple whom Jesus loved.
All this strikes us as very odd; it is certainly not the way we go
about things today. It is, nevertheless, a possible explanation of
the fact of the four gospels and, some would say, the best
explanation so far available. On reflection, we realize that at
different periods of history, conventions about writing books
have been different from what they are today; and that Christians of the first and second centuries, in spite of what distin-
guished them from their contemporaries, were in most respects
people of their time, operating within the customs and conventions that were shared by everybody. It would have been strange
if it had not been so; our self-knowledge assures us that it is the
same with us.

There will be many points at which the way John writes
surprises us, because we belong to a very different world from

his; but his aim and purpose in writing his book may not seem so strange, because, we hope, it is possible to a far greater extent to share John's faith and religious outlook than to approve of his method of writing. Certainly his book has been much used and very highly regarded for nearly nineteen centuries, and this estimation is not dependent on any one opinion about its authorship, date, or relationship to the events it purports to record.

John says that Jesus did many other signs in the presence of his disciples that he has not included; this may be an oblique reference to the other gospels, which all contain many more miracle-stories than John. It is perhaps a way of forestalling criticism of his book; he is saying that what he has written is enough for his readers in respect of the purpose for which he has written, that they should have faith and receive life. He could have no higher aim than this. It looks, therefore, as though he meant his book to be read on its own and by itself, not as a supplement to other gospels. None of the evangelists does in fact refer the reader to the other books for further information, in the way that the author of Kings, for example, sends us to the Books of the Chronicles of the Kings of Israel and Judah. Late in the second century a bishop in France argued that to be an orthodox Christian you must use all four gospels, and that it was a mark of being a heretic to use only one; but it had not been so always; it could not have been, unless all four books had been written at the same time, and that seems impossible. At first, churches had one gospel, not four; they revised and re-wrote earlier gospels, because they believed they could improve on what was there. The bishop who said you must have all four was being the innovator, and the heretics that admitted only one gospel were the conservatives. To read these four books, even now, we must read them as they were meant to be read, and written to be used: one by one, as though the one we are attending to were for this moment the only one there was.

All four gospels, it seems, except for the first, came into existence because people were dissatisfied with previous attempts to write a gospel; and this sense of dissatisfaction seems to have been particularly strong in the case of the writing of John. What we need to do now is to find out what were the specific areas in which John felt the need for change and improvement.

One way to start to do this is to read the book straight through from beginning to end, as most books should be read, though for some strange reason we do not usually do it with gospels. Anyone who does this, and has some acquaintance with the other three gospels, immediately senses a change of atmosphere in John: there is a different vocabulary; a different texture to the material; almost, one might be tempted to say, a different religion. In the other three gospels, Jesus had preached the kingdom of God (or, in Matthew, the kingdom of heaven); he had taught his disciples how to be ready for the coming of the Son of man, for the last judgement and the life of the age to come on the new earth that God would make when all evil had been removed from the present world. The whole of this way of thinking is missing from John's gospel: the kingdom of God is scarcely mentioned and plays no part in the way John thinks and writes; there is no waiting for the Son of man to come or being ready for the judgement; there is no expectation of a renewed earth, Paradise restored, because now the intention is that the believers will be taken to the Father's house with its many rooms, and the world, as far as we can see, will be abandoned; there is no future for it.

John is replacing a religion of hope for a new age that will come on the earth (such as is prayed for in the prayer, Thy kingdom come, thy will be done, on earth) with a different religion of union with Christ and God; this is what he means by eternal life, and it begins now. This fundamental shift from hope to union, from the future to the present (one might say, to use dangerous and difficult words, from apocalyptic to mysticism), explains why it is we feel that we are in a different atmosphere when we pass from the other three gospels to John. The present displaces the future; Christ and union with him now displaces the kingdom of God for which we were praying; believing, loving and abiding in Christ displace living in obedience to the teaching of Jesus and following him as we wait for his coming in glory.

The changes that John made had advantages and disadvantages. For example, it was an advantage that there was now no longer any problem about the end of the world; the return of Christ had not come in the way and at the time that Mark, Matthew and Luke had led their readers to expect. John's new formulation of Christian faith took the waiting out of wanting and gave immediate access to Jesus and God in the present; the future could be left to take care of itself. But the disadvantage that resulted from this was a weakening of the sense of community that came from sharing the experience of waiting together and praying together for the kingdom to come and for God's will to be done. John's way of expressing faith was highly individualistic, not in the sense that he was unlike the other New Testament writers, but in the sense that the stress was on the union of the individual believer with Jesus, and with God. At an important and revealing point in John's book, where the difference between what we may call the old religion and the new is being discussed, Jesus replies to Judas' question about the manifestation of God that it will not be to the world, but to the one who loves him and keeps his word; the believer will be the dwelling-place of the Father and the Son; this is the final state, as John presents it: the mutual indwelling of God, Christ and the believer; I in you and you in me. There is, of course, the new commandment, and the believers are to love one another; but John does not show, as Paul had shown, that disciples need one another and depend on each other; in John, they are not seen as members of a body, but as sheep known individually by the shepherd, or as branches dealt with by the husbandman one by one. And the consequence of this is, as we shall see, that there is very little in John about the corporate or institutional aspect of Christianity, the church, the ministry or the sacraments.

A further disadvantage of the new expression of the faith that John was introducing was that it abandoned the idea of the earth as our future home, the place where God would rule; so there was no need, as John saw it, to act responsibly for the world, to care for it and to look forward to its future release from the bondage of corruption to share in the liberty of the glory of the children of God. John could fairly be described as other-worldly, whereas Paul could not, nor the other evangelists, nor the author of The Revelation.

The positive and negative aspects of John's great achievement will become more clear as we read his book; before we do that, however, there are two points we must attend to, because if we do not, John will scarcely make any sense at all. He assumes an attitude to life as we have it now, apart from the insights that are provided by faith, that we may or may not share; but unless we see what it is he assumes, we shall almost certainly miss much of what he is saying. John's experience of life is that it is not fulfilling or satisfying, but inadequate and disappointing. This can be seen most clearly from the selection of miracle-stories that he has made for inclusion in his book; they all portray the failure of life as we have it here and now to meet the expectations that it arouses in us, or to satisfy the hopes it creates. It is like a wedding-party at which the wine has run out, or a child at the point of death, or a lame man who cannot get healing, or people who are hungry on a mountain or afraid at sea in a boat, or a person who suffers from congenital blindness, or a corpse in a tomb. These are the situations John has chosen to symbolize human life as we experience it, in its inadequacy and tragedy; it calls for weeping. But Jesus is shown, in each case, as the one who brings release and salvation: he rescues those who are on the brink of extinction and gives life to those who would otherwise be dead.

Because John has presented Jesus in this way, his book will not make sense to anyone who finds life in this world all that it should be. If there is nothing wrong, it is nonsense to present Jesus as the one who puts everything right. Just as John did not think that the earlier gospels were good enough, so he did not think that life as we have it now was satisfactory. He wanted more, and better. The book is an uncomfortable book, because the author of it was a man who was not satisfied with things as they are. His readers sense his conviction that life is empty.

The other point that we shall have to consider briefly before we begin to read his book is one that he never raises explicitly; but if we do not attend to it now, we shall find John's teaching strange and difficult to accept. John clearly thought that the world God had made was imperfect and contained within it negative elements, which he refers to as darkness, and lies, and death. He also believed that the one through whom God had made the world had entered it, to bring to the human creatures a new kind of existence, which he refers to as eternal life; and that this was available through faith in Jesus, union with him, and abiding in him. Not everyone, however, has this faith; some are overcome by the darkness, hate the light, and seem to have no opportunity of ever being able to believe and receive the gift that Jesus offers.

There are many problems for us in this, but one that we need to attend to immediately is: Why could not God have made the final state, in which creatures are in union with him, at the beginning? Why did he have to go the long way round, of creating a world that was incomplete, and then coming into it himself (he was in the world, and the world was made by him)? The answer which seems most compatible with John's ideas is that what God values is the individual human being; that God respects faith and love and uses them as the means of salvation. He relates to men and women as love, and looks for love as the response that makes union with himself a possibility. This state of affairs could not have been created out of nothing and imposed unilaterally; there had to be the duality of lover and beloved, and the freedom of the creature to turn to God. The hiddenness of God was essential, and the imperfection of the world, in order that there might be the conditions and circumstances in which love and faith might be exercised freely.

In thinking like this, however, we have passed out of the world of John, and asked questions that he never dealt with, so far as we know. Nor, as we shall see, is this way of expressing the over-all plan of God entirely consistent with much that John says. He does, however, say quite clearly that he writes in order that we may believe, and have life: God has therefore created a situation in which faith is required, in order that we may receive God's final gift.

How to use this book

This is a book about a book, but it is not intended that it should be a substitute for the book it is about, as though one could read this book and dispense with John's gospel. One could no more do that than read the concert programme notes and leave before the music began, or study a travel book instead of travelling.

Therefore in order to use this book properly, it will be absolutely essential for the reader to have a copy of John's gospel open alongside it, and to read the sections of the gospel as they are being discussed here. The best method in fact is to read the section of John's gospel first (the chapter numbers and the verse numbers are printed at the beginning of each section), then to read the relevant passage in this book, and finally to read the gospel text for a second time.

Even before this, there is another exercise which is strongly recommended and has already been mentioned in this Introduction: set aside a period of two hours, and read John's gospel straight through in one sitting from beginning to end. We hear gospels read to us in such short extracts, and we attend so little to which author we are hearing, that the result is that we do not know what is in any one of them, and what is not.

The aim of this book is only to illuminate John's gospel; it is not to make that book redundant. There will always be far more in the original text than any one expositor can draw from it. What is wanted and hoped for is that the text of John's gospel will reveal itself to the reader; this, and nothing else. The exposition of the text in this book aims only a putting the reader in a position in which John's text itself will illuminate him; and it attempts to do this by suggesting ways of looking and questions to ask, and by pointing to what seems to the expositor to be there for others to see and hear. The function of the expositor is always temporary and terminal: he must decrease, in order that the text may increase in its power and effect upon the reader.

There are many translations of the gospel, easily available, and it does not matter much which is used. (The translation that was used in the writing of this book was the Revised Standard Version (RSV, 2nd edition, 1971).) There is much to be said for reading a translation that is unfamiliar. One of the enemies of Biblical study is familiarity, and it can be deadly.

Finding the way through John

1.1–18 The prologue

John begins his book with a passage that is unlike anything that he writes elsewhere in the gospel, or that occurs in any other gospel. It is of a semi-poetic nature, and its subject is the relation between Jesus Christ, who is the central character of the book, and the creation and salvation of the world.

The first words of the gospel recall the first words of the Scriptures, the beginning of Genesis; and this sets up in the reader's mind a comparison between what happened in creation and what happens when there is faith. The life which came into existence through the Word of God in the beginning contained within it the possibility of death; but what has now happened, through the same Word of God, is that a better life has been made available which can never die: it is the Word himself who has brought it into the world, and he is it. Again, at the beginning there was light and darkness, day and night; but in this new creation there will be no more night and no more darkness.

The human beings whom the Word has made refuse to admit that they are creatures who have a creator; they live a lie, and live in the darkness. In order to recognize and believe in the Word when he comes into the world, they need the help of one who will point him out to them; and this begins in the activity of John the Baptist, who is the first witness to Jesus and the origin of all the subsequent witnesses, so that everyone who believes owes his faith, ultimately, to him.

The book begins, then, in a way that reminds the reader of the beginning of Genesis, the first book of Moses. John will have much to say about the relationship between Jesus and Judaism as his book continues; at this point, however, he makes it clear that Judaism is the home of Christianity, and that the Jews did not believe in Jesus. To believe is to be the object of God's action, a receiver rather than a doer; the best way to describe faith is to use the language of birth, because in birth one is acted upon; no one is the cause of his own conception.

God made the world by his Word, and this same Word has now appeared in flesh, as a human being, within his creation; he is the Father's only Son, and the Baptist points to him as the one who is far greater than himself, because he is the bringer of the final gift of God to his creatures; that is, the grace that is the true and final union of creatures with God through Jesus Christ. This is something far superior to what was given through the law of Judaism; it is God's ultimate gift of himself to his creatures, and it is an expression of his unsurpassable love.

1.19–51 *The testimony of John and its effect*

The evangelist has already told us about the man sent from God whose name was John; he mentioned him near the beginning of the prologue, and he comes at the beginning of the other gospels also. All four evangelists are true to the facts in this respect: the first followers of Jesus would have been seen at the time as a break-away movement from the larger group who followed John the Baptist. But John's book begins with the testimony of the Baptist, not so much because John is interested in recording what happened, as because faith is response to witness, and all witness has its origin in John. This was also the view of Mark and Matthew and Luke: John had declared Jesus to be the one who was to be believed and followed, the one who was greater than himself. Mark, Matthew and, to a lesser extent, Luke had interpreted John as Elijah returned from heaven to prepare Israel for the final hour; but John does not follow them in this respect, perhaps because he is moving away from end-of-the-world ways of thinking; the Baptist is now to be seen as only the voice that prepares the way of the Lord; he has no other importance, and has no independent status. This is typical of John's way of seeing things: the only value anything has is determined by its relation to Jesus; the Father has given everything into his hand, and Judaism, scripture, the Baptist and the disciples of Jesus are only significant in so far as they bear witness to him.

It is in accordance with this that the water-baptism administered by John is in this gospel no more than an occasion on which and by which Jesus is recognized; it is not referred to as a baptism of repentance for the forgiveness of sins, as in Mark; here, it will be Jesus who will take away the sin of the world, not John, or baptism in the Jordan.

Jesus is revealed to John through the descent of the Spirit as a dove from heaven; John sees this, and declares Jesus to be the Son of God, the one who will baptize with the Holy Spirit.

The evangelist is using the traditional account of the baptism of Jesus, which we can read in the other gospels; but his way of telling the story completely alters the emphasis from what it had been in the earlier versions. John never in fact says that Jesus was baptized, only that the Spirit descended and remained on him. The contrast between John baptizing with water and Jesus baptizing with the Holy Spirit suggests a difference between the visible and material sacrament of baptism and the new order that is now beginning in which there will not be the same sort of visibility and materiality. We shall see, again and again, that this evangelist is uneasy about the way sacraments are being presented in the church in his time; he is critical of a system that is already developing, and part of his purpose in writing a new and very different gospel seems to be to break away from the current trend.

The story of the two disciples who heard the Baptist's testimony, followed Jesus, asked him where he was staying, received the answer Come and see, and came and stayed, is a piece of carefully constructed ambiguity. Almost every word has two senses: to hear and to come are to believe; to stay or abide is a key term in the johannine vocabulary, since the Son abides in the Father, and the disciple in the Son; to see is to receive the final gift of God, the vision of the glory of the Father and the Son which is eternal life. So the story of Andrew and his companion is the story of faith, which begins when testimony is received and Jesus is followed, and ends in the union of the disciple with God and his Son. What happened to these two disciples symbolizes and prefigures what will happen to all believers who follow Jesus.

A notable feature of this section of the gospel is the use made here of titles applied to Jesus: the Lamb of God, the Messiah, the King of Israel. These titles are accepted, but with the comment and on the condition that the reader is to see greater things than these. It is as if the evangelist were pointing beyond what had been believed in the past, and the expressions that had become traditional, to a new, deeper and more startling understanding of Jesus; he is not to be thought of as a human being with supernatural insight, but as the mediator between God and humanity, the ladder by which God's grace is brought into the world and the redeemed ascend to God; he is, as John will say later in the book, the one and only way to God. The traditional titles, John seems to be saying, did not adequately express this.

The section is marked by a movement from the Baptist to Jesus, from water to spirit, from expectation to fulfilment. Instead of the law given through Moses we are being invited to receive the grace and truth that come with Jesus Christ. Though he comes into the world after the Baptist, and after Moses, he is greater than both of them, and existed before them, because he is the Word through whom all things were made. He has now come to complete what he made by uniting believers to God in a way that will surpass anything that the law could do or even suggest. God's new gift exceeds all that he had done before.

2.1–25 The wine and the temple

The previous passage, ending with the promise of greater things, led us to expect something extraordinary to happen next, and John does not disappoint us. He tells us immediately of two events in which Jesus was the central character, one of which happened in Galilee, and the other in Jerusalem; in both of them we are led to understand that life as it is at present is to be replaced by something that will be far better: richer, greater and totally satisfying.

The two events are the wedding at Cana and the cleansing of the temple in Jerusalem. In both of them, John's account of what happened must be read as a symbol of what Jesus has brought into the world and made available: that new and final gift of God which is real and eternal life in union with him. John indicates the way in which he wants us to look at these stories by calling the miracle at Cana, not a miracle, but a sign; that is, an event that signifies something other than itself. In John, everything points, and points to Jesus.

These two events that John has placed side by side at the beginning of his account of the ministry of Jesus will be followed by passages consisting of conversation and discussion; and we shall find that this will be a characteristic of the way John has put his book together. He tends to put narratives first and then to use discussion-passages to throw light on the meaning of what he has already written. It may be that the reader will feel that the exposition of these first two incidents over-presses the details of the stories, and that meanings are being found that were never intended. But when we come on to the discussion-passages in chapters 3 and 4, we shall, I hope, see that John had intended us to take the stories as allegories, and had meant the reader to reflect on the details in order to understand the difference that Christ's coming has made and be amazed at the glory of God.

The first sign is linked to the previous section by the statement that it happened on the third day. The evangelist had said that grace and truth came through Jesus Christ, the Baptist had testified that Jesus was greater than himself, and Jesus had promised a vision of the ultimate reality and of the means by which the reader could participate in it. Now, at the marriage of Cana, the sign which Jesus performs points towards this new and final gift of God.

There is not enough wine; that describes the human situation apart from Christ. It is not that there is no joy in life, but that the joy there is leads us to want more, and that is not available. Everything is under sentence of death; so all the good things in the world, such as love, friendship, pleasure, art, health, knowledge, will be destroyed; it will all end in tears. We experience life as expectations that have been raised only to be disappointed; and the story of a party where there is some drink but not enough is an image that fits. The mother of Jesus plays a particular rôle in the story: she is aware of the problem, and she expresses faith in Jesus as the one who will solve it; but she can go no further than this, and the words of Jesus to her mark out and define the difference between them. She represents Israel, as the matrix in which Christianity has been conceived: salvation is from the Jews. What she asks Jesus to do is to give the wine that symbolizes eternal life; but he can only do this by laying down his life in order that others may receive it, and the hour for it to happen has not yet come. The only thing that Jesus can do now is perform the sign, not mediate the reality itself; and he does this by the production of the better wine in vast quantities. This takes place in the jars that had been placed there for an entirely different purpose, the Jewish rites of purification; so we are made to recall that grace and truth take the place of the law, and that Jesus displaces Moses from the position of authority. There is also a characteristically Johannine misunderstanding on the part of the steward who supposes that the bridegroom at the wedding is responsible for the good wine that has now been made available. Jesus himself, we shall learn later, is the real bridegroom, and it is he who has brought the better thing, at the end instead of at the beginning. The glory of Jesus which is revealed in this story is not the power to change water into wine, but to give eternal life; and the disciples, who have tasted what he gives, believe in him.

There is no story in the other gospels closely similar to John's first sign, and it may be that the evangelist's faith in Jesus as the bringer of life has created the story to be the means of its expression. But in the case of the other event recorded in this chapter, the cleansing of the temple in Jerusalem, John is using material that was also used by the other evangelists, though John is never content to take a story over as it was, and use it without alteration; he has re-told the incident in the temple to make his own points, and he has put it at the beginning of the ministry, rather than at the end, which is where the other evangelists had placed it.

What needs to be removed from the temple is the material for offering sacrifices and the means for acquiring it. The Father's house is not to be a house of trade, because the worship which God requires is not to be performed through the use of oxen, sheep and pigeons. Jesus' zeal for the temple will lead to his death, but his death will inaugurate a new order in which there will be no more temples of stone, just as there will be no more animal sacrifices; every believer will be the place where God dwells and where he is worshipped.

The Jews, who in this gospel act out the rôle of unbelievers, ask for a sign, by which they mean a miracle that will authenticate Jesus as the agent of God with the power to alter the law as it had been given through Moses. Jesus says that the sign will be the resurrection; what is happening now anticipates what will become effective only then. But he uses the expression, *this temple*, in such a way that the Jews think he is talking about Herod's temple, in which they are standing; in fact, John says, he means his body, which they will destroy at his command, and he will raise up; yet the Jerusalem temple will also be destroyed, by the Romans; and Judaism, as John believes, will surrender its legitimacy because of the coming of its fulfilment. We should also notice that the date when this took place is given: it was Passover, John says; and Passover will be the time when Jesus himself is put to death as the Lamb of God who redeems the world and thereby abolishes the sacrificial system.

Finally, John says that many believed in Jesus because of the signs that he did, but that Jesus did not welcome such faith. He is the saviour, and the saviour knows those whom he saves, and those who do not believe in him. To believe in Jesus because he can turn water into wine, for example, is not what John calls faith; it is only to believe in Jesus as a miracle-worker and no more, because it mistakes the sign for what it signifies. Throughout this gospel there is a critical attitude to miracles; they are recorded (though fewer of them than in any other gospel), but they are not to be over-valued; they are only important in so far as the reader sees through them.

3.1–21 A new beginning

The man who wrote this extraordinary gospel had a strong sense of humour which appears again and again in his writing. The kind of humour that he had and used might be described as vicious: he presents his story as involving two sorts of people, those who can see, and those who are blind; to those who can see, amongst whom he includes himself, the blind look ridiculous as they stumble and fall about, not knowing where they are going or what has hit them.

Nicodemus, for example, who is introduced to us as an authoritative representative of Judaism, is treated as a buffoon in the eyes of John's readers. His opening statement is entirely mistaken, and a total misunderstanding of the situation, all the more ridiculous by being expressed so pompously. He addresses Jesus as Rabbi, which is always in this book a mark of the speaker's ignorance and need of enlightenment; he says that Jesus is a teacher come from God, whereas he is the Word of God, through whom all things were made; he accepts the signs as the evidence that God is with Jesus, but this is to make a double mistake, because faith that is based on the signs understood as miracles is inadequate, they must be seen as pointers to Jesus as the Word, and because it is not the case that Jesus is one with whom God is present; the Word is God. Nicodemus has spoken as a Jew, that is, in this book, as one who does not believe. He has tried to contain Jesus within Jewish categories. As John sees it, this cannot be done. New wine needs new skins.

Jesus rejects the attempt to describe him in this way because it is inadequate. There is no continuity between Judaism and Christianity, but a gulf, and there has to be a new beginning. Here, and only here in John's gospel, the key term from the other gospels is used, twice over: the kingdom of God. The context shows that the point that is being made is not that the kingdom of God is an expression that Christians can easily retain, but that if one thinks in the Jewish way of a time to come when God will rule and his will only will be done, it is still not possible to see this age or to enter this realm without a completely fresh start; and the suggestion is that those who have made this fresh start will no longer use expressions such as the kingdom of God. But what is far more important is that the new beginning that is called for is one that no one can make for himself, because it is like being born. Grace is God's gift, and he always retains the initiative, as the giver; no one can manipulate God or manoeuvre him into action.

The reference to water recalls baptism, the sacrament of Christian initiation; but the context makes it clear that baptism should not be thought of as though God had surrendered his initiative to others, so that they could dispense God's grace as they wished; they can no more control who will and who will not be born from above than they can tame the wind or understand its ways. (Wind and Spirit are the same word in Greek, and have the same property of mystery.) To one who lives within a religious system that is closed and offers its benefits in return for obedience to its regulations, this openness and incomprehensibility is puzzling and threatening; so Nicodemus is left in confusion. He cannot make the connection between the analogy of the wind and the way in which God's Spirit works. There is indeed only one way to the new beginning, and that is faith in Jesus, but this faith is itself God's gift. Moses had provided a symbol of Jesus in the bronze serpent which healed those who had been bitten by snakes; what Moses did prefigured what Jesus will do: he will give life to the dying, by giving himself up to death.

The remainder of this section explains the reason why there is and must be the distinction between flesh and Spirit, Judaism and Christianity, blindness and sight, unbelief and faith. One might have thought it was so because God was uncaring; but in fact it is just the opposite of this; the situation is as it is because God loves the world and in this love has sent the Son to bring eternal life into it. This life, as we have already seen and shall see again later, is the Son himself, and not a gift that can be detached from him; the only way in which we can have life is through having the Son; that is, through believing in him and being united to him. Not to believe is to miss the gift of life. Not to believe has its origin in something else; namely, in the refusal of the creature to accept its creatureliness and in its love of the darkness and the lie that it is its own God. Evil is rejection of the truth that God is God and that he made the world and all that is in it; the attempt to live as though there were no God is darkness.

The question that John leaves us with at this point in his book is whether God, who is love, can draw everyone out of their chosen darkness into the light. Sometimes John seems to despair; but at other times he is far more hopeful that all will be saved. The more he emphasises God's initiative and grace, the more hope there is; the less he stresses the human contribution to salvation, the less reason there is to despair. We may well find his doctrine of election and predestination difficult to accept; but it could be seen as the most hopeful part of his teaching: if love is in control, then all shall be well.

3.22–36 *The last testimony of John*

In these early sections of his book, the evangelist is concerned among other things to make it clear to us what he sees as the proper relationship between Judaism and Christianity. He has given us Nicodemus as a representative of one point of view, that of those who want to incorporate Jesus within the limitations and ideas of the religion of Moses and the law; and he has shown us that this is not possible: the new wine bursts the skins of the old order. The only appropriate attitude for Judaism to adopt towards Christiany, as John sees it, is now stated again in the final words of the Baptist.

He begins with a clear statement of the utmost importance, that God himself is in control, and that no one can manipulate him by attempting to act a part in the world that has not been assigned to him by God. The Baptist speaks on behalf of Judaism as it should be, when he says that he is not that which is final, but is only the preparation for it and the witness to it: he is the friend of the bridegroom, not the groom himself. The rôle of the Baptist, the law, the synagogue, the temple, is to wane, now that the reality to which they point and for which they had waited has arrived.

Jesus is contrasted with the Baptist and with all the other forms of preparation and prophecy and witness of which the Baptist is the final and complete example, as heaven is contrasted with earth. To believe Jesus is to believe God, because Jesus is God's final messenger and is to be understood in a way that puts him in a different class from all previous messengers, such as the prophets of Israel; they spoke through the Spirit and were inspired by God, but only in part and fragmentarily; Jesus, on the other hand, has received the gift of the Spirit in totality, so that he is the one, final and incomparable agent of God with full and complete authority to act for God. The result of this is that anyone who believes in Jesus is united to him and receives the gift which God wills to give to the world, eternal life.

4.1–42 *The saviour of the world*

John now writes the first of his longer narratives which are so characteristic of his gospel; there are no comparable stories in the other three. With great skill, he develops the ideas and beliefs that he wants to share with his readers. Nicodemus had been a purely negative character, demonstrating the need for faith through an account of one who did not have it. The Baptist had been the final witness to the new order, but he was not himself a member of it or a follower of Jesus. So for this third section John needs an instance of one who will become both a believer and a witness. The remarkable thing is that John chooses a woman for this rôle, and not a Jewish woman, or indeed just any woman, but a Samaritan woman; he could scarcely have made a more unexpected choice, because Samaritans were hated and despised by Jews, and women were regarded as practically non-persons. To confound the moralist in us even more, the woman who is presented to us now, to be the third in the series that had Nicodemus and John the Baptist as numbers one and two, is a woman whose married life is far from exemplary.

In this story, Judaism is represented by the well that Jacob gave to Joseph; and the new gift of eternal life is referred to, in contrast with this well, as living or flowing water; the misunderstanding of the ambiguity is pursued in a way that we have already come to appreciate; it is without parallel in the other gospels, and a clear sign of johannine authorship. The woman is made to state the Christian position without realizing what she is doing, when she asks whether Jesus is greater than the patriarch Jacob; and she also unintentionally confesses the inferiority of Jacob to Jesus when she says that it was not only Jacob and his sons who drank from the well, but his cattle too. The benefits of Judaism are thus devalued to the level of the merely animal; John, in contrast with the Old Testament and Paul, sees God's interest as applying only to human beings.

God's final gift is greater than anything that is experienced in the world; it takes the receiver out of the repeated cycle of temporary satisfaction followed by renewed need. Eternal life surpasses every good thing that it is possible to receive from the world, and detaches those who accept it from the world of time. The woman does not understand this; she can see that she is being offered something that is better than what she has, and that it is to be greatly desired; but she imagines it as though it belonged to this world, and she supposes that if she had it she would not need to draw water from the well.

In order to shift her from her misunderstanding, Jesus changes the subject. As the Baptist had said, Jesus is the bridegroom; he asks her therefore to call her husband, and we wait to see whether she will recognize that the one who is speaking to her, her maker, is he. She replies that she has no husband, so the question whether she will perceive who Jesus is remains. Now it is her turn to change the subject, and she brings us back to the second of the two introductory signs, the cleansing of the temple in Jerusalem. Since it is clear to the woman that Jesus is a prophet with supernatural knowledge, he should, she thinks, be able to solve the question that had divided Jews from Samaritans: Where was God's temple? On Mount Gerizim, or on Mount Zion? The answer is that in the new order there will be no sacred buildings; true worship will be internal, invisible and spiritual. This was why Jesus had ordered the removal of the sacrificial animals and the money-changers from the temple. Here again we see John's protest against the way Christianity was developing into a system of churches and sacraments, and his understanding of it as individualistic and mystical.

Notice the contrast between the disciples and the woman: she has greater insight than they; she bears witness to her fellow Samaritans and is the sower of the harvest. It is because of the faith of the Samaritans that we are now able to see that Jesus is the saviour, not only of the Jews, but of the world. Thus by his use of the figure of the Samaritan woman, John is returning to a very early insight in the gospel tradition that was always in danger of being obscured, that Jesus came to invite sinners, not the righteous; the gospel is biased in favour of the outsider and the wicked, because it is good news of God's love, and those who apparently have least claim to it will therefore see it as it is more clearly.

4.43–54 *Life for the dying*

Jesus returns to Galilee where he had performed his first sign, and another follows at Capernaum; again it is a sign pointing to what he brings into the world and makes available to those who believe in him.

This miracle-story is similar in many respects to one of the very few accounts of healing that Matthew and Luke have in common but that Mark does not record. A father comes to Jesus to ask for the healing of his son who is sick and near to death. The man is a Gentile and the healing is performed at a distance. The other evangelists draw attention to the fact that this is one of the few instances of Jesus healing someone who was not a Jew, but John makes nothing of that point; he raises instead the question of the relationship between signs and wonders and faith.

The friction between Jesus and the official arises out of the duality of the story: on one level it is a narrative of a healing; but on another level it is a symbol of faith, and of life through faith. The official is a character in the narrative who simply asks for the healing of his son; but he is rebuked by Jesus as though he had demanded a miracle in order to believe. He quite naturally objects to being treated in this way, and brings Jesus back to his, and his son's, immediate situation. Jesus then answers the man's request, just as he performed the miracle at Cana for which his mother had asked, after a preliminary delay. The official takes what Jesus has said on trust, and returns home to find that the cure had happened at the moment when Jesus had spoken; the result is that he and his household become believers; that is to say, they move from the narrative-level onto that of the symbol: the sign has led them into faith, and the life-giving word of Jesus has had its effect on them all. Jesus' rebuke is now seen to have been a true prediction: they have seen the sign and they have believed.

5.1–47 *The Son gives life*

In the early part of his gospel, John follows a pattern, which he repeats again and again: incidents which are signs as to who Jesus is and what he is bringing into the world are followed by speeches or discussions or arguments which comment on the signs and bring out their meaning. At this point the pattern is very clear; we have just had a sign in Galilee, and now we are to have a sign in Jerusalem, just as at the beginning of the book we had first the miracle at Cana and then the cleansing of the temple; and in both cases, the signs are followed by discussion-passages. The healing of the boy at the point of death through the words, Your son will live, has announced the theme for this second cycle of signs and speeches, and it will continue in the healing of the lame man in Jerusalem, and in the argument that follows.

Jesus is the bringer of life; this is the whole message of John's book, and it is indicated here by means of the story of a man who had been waiting thirty-eight years by a pool to be healed in its waters. His problem is that he has lost the desire to be well, and has become institutionalized; he accepts sickness as a way of life, and makes excuses for himself to conceal his real situation; he blames others for his condition. The healing words of Jesus recall a miracle-story in the other gospels in which a paralysed man is let down through the roof. Here in John, however, a new twist is added, by the statement that the healing took place on the sabbath, so that the sick man should not be carrying his pallet; and this sparks off the controversy between Jesus and the

Jews. Jesus' defence is that God's work does not cease even on the sabbath; he continues, for instance, to sustain the world by giving it life. Jesus is God's Son, and he too works on the sabbath; that is the justification for his healing the man at the pool on this particular day of the week. This leads to even greater opposition from the Jews, who suppose that Jesus is making a blasphemous claim for himself by justifying his actions through an appeal to God's action. They suppose that he is making himself equal to God. The question is, What is the relationship between Jesus and God? This is the subject of Jesus' speech, and it is clear that by this point in the book it is a subject that cannot be postponed any longer.

We need to have no doubt about the impression that the ministry, death and resurrection of Jesus made on his followers; the evidence is that people who had previously been strict monotheists, and had repeated daily the confession that there is only one God, found themselves forced by the situation in which they were living to speak of the Father and the Son, and thus introduce a duality into their conception of one God; this caused grave offence to other Jews who did not share their faith. Our present section of John's book is to be seen against this background. It attempts to give an answer to the question, How can we believe in Jesus as the giver of life, and still believe that there is one God? What we shall see is that John and those who thought like him were dissatisfied with the view that Jesus was the last of the prophets, or a man on whom the spirit of God had come; John was moving towards a faith in Jesus that was to be expressed later in terms of the doctrines of the Holy Trinity and the Incarnation.

Notice, however, that the speech of Jesus begins with a negative statement, denying that the Son can act independently of the Father; he is wholly obedient to the Father and entirely dependent on him. What has been seen so far in John's book is only the beginning of what will emerge later; healing is only a sign of the real, final and incomparable life that the Son will give. Just as there can be no greater gift than this, so God can have no greater agent that the one through whom this gift is given; the Father has bestowed all authority on him, so that the honour due to the Son is equal to the honour that is due to the Father; and the gift of the Son to those who hear him and believe in him is eternal life. Moreover, because the Son is both the giver of life and the judge of the world, his gift anticipates the final judgement, because it is made now, before the end of the world; and thus it abolishes judgement for the believer: those who believe have already entered into life; God's acceptance of them has been demonstrated by this.

Thus what Paul and the writers of the other three gospels looked forward to as future, the life of the age to come, John understands as present. The believer need not wait for anything except the gift of faith; when faith is given, the tomb is opened, and the believer comes out of it, like a dead man coming to life.

The Son acts in total obedience to the Father, and the Father for his part bears witness to the Son. So the witness of John the Baptist is not to be thought of as though it were only that of another human being, and therefore partial and imperfect; John was a man, but he was sent by God. God also bears witness to Jesus through the signs and speech of Jesus, and these too show who he is to those with faith to believe in him. The Jews, however, who have so misunderstood Jesus that they persecute him, have not even grasped the purpose of the scriptures. They have made a religion out of what was meant to be only a prediction; they stop at the sign instead of going on in the direction in which it points. Their error is the same as that which John finds among believers, who use Christian faith to establish a system of church and ministry and sacraments as if there were no Son who gives life, but only an impersonal and institutional religion. This error, the institutionalization of faith, is the result of the desire for glory: not the desire to give glory to God or to love him, but the longing to receive glory from others, because the only object of love is oneself. Moses, who gave the law, is the witness to Jesus; his books are full of the symbols and predictions that point to Jesus; the brazen serpent, for example.

Those who do not read the scriptures in this way will not be able to believe the Son when he bears true witness to himself.

We talk about the benefit of hindsight, and this is the method that is used here by John. The historian who wants to understand the past as it understood itself would not agree with John that Moses and the Baptist foretold Jesus, or that Jesus bore witness to himself. John sees the truth of Jesus everywhere; it is God's testimony to his Son. He writes as an enthusiast, not as a precise and technical scholar.

6.1–71 *I am the bread of life*

The interpretation of this chapter is crucial for the understanding of this gospel. It is a book that sets out to correct previous traditions and to alter the direction in which the churches were going, and in this chapter we have an opportunity to see the main points of difference between John, his contemporaries and his predecessors. We have seen that he avoided saying that Jesus was baptized by John the Baptist; and that he ascribed rebirth more to the Spirit than to a sacrament. We shall notice later that he will not include any account of the institution of the eucharist on the night of the betrayal, and in this he will differ not only from Mark, Matthew and Luke, but also from an earlier tradition quoted by Paul when he was writing to the Corinthians. Just as John had used the language of baptism to describe the way in which the Holy Spirit works, so now he uses the language of the eucharist to describe the way in which Christ's death brings life to those who believe in him. We can only suppose that John has chosen to do this in protest against what he sees as the misuse of sacraments; they can be turned into objects and things in such a way that the personal relationship between Christ and the believer is obscured and forgotten. John's whole enterprise in writing his book may be seen as an attempt to prevent this from happening. He wants to say: There is Jesus Christ; there is the person who believes in Jesus Christ, and this person is a gift given by the Father to the Son; but there is no third thing, to be thought of as the means by which they meet, or the agency through which they are associated with each other. The first of the I AM sayings (when Jesus identifies himself with images of life), which comes in this chapter, rules out the possibility of there being such a third thing: I am the bread of life excludes the suggestion that there are three distinct realities: Christ, the believer and the sacramental bread. There are only two: the believer, and Christ who is the bread. What others assert about the eucharistic bread and wine, John ascribes to Jesus himself; this is the sense of the johannine I AM.

From this chapter on to the end of chapter 17, John will make the point repeatedly that the gift which Jesus has come into the world to bring is himself, and not anything that can be separated from him, or possessed without possessing him. The I AM sayings do this. John is thus underlining, with almost exaggerated emphasis, the personal nature of Christian faith and its working. Christ's gift to the believer is himself, and there is no way of having his gift except through the relationship with him which is faith.

In this section, Jesus is presented as the bread that must be eaten in order that there may be life; and to eat a person, in scriptural usage, is to be his enemy and to destroy him; Israel's enemies eat up God's people like bread and Christ is both victim and life-giver. The section begins with a reference to Passover, the time when Jesus will lay down his life, and ends with a reference to Judas Iscariot who betrayed him.

As in previous sections of the gospel, John uses material that he has taken either from the other gospels or from the tradition on which the other evangelists also drew; and here the parallels are closer than anywhere else in the book. The feeding of the five thousand is followed by the walking on the lake in Mark and Matthew, and the statement of faith made by Peter is prominent in all three gospels, Mark, Matthew and Luke. But, as always, nothing is exactly the same in John as it is in the other three; he has adapted the material to his own purposes and added to it considerably; we can see his hand in the use he makes of ambiguity and misunderstanding, in the account of the conflict between Jesus and the Jews, and the theology that finds expression here.

For the third and final time, John repeats the pattern of two signs followed by discussion and speech; after this, the two remaining signs will be given separately. Notice in John's version of the feeding of the multitude that it is Jesus who takes the initiative, not the disciples; he knows what he will do: he will perform the sign that he is the saviour of the world, the one who can satisfy their hunger for real life. Those who are fed are portrayed as people who have only a rudimentary faith that is inadequate and imperfect; they have come to Jesus because of the signs, and they see in him nothing more than a prophet, like Elisha for example whose miraculous feeding of a hundred men is recalled in John's story through the detail that it was barley loaves that were used. Their reaction to the miracle is to make Jesus king by force, and this shows that they have not yet understood who he is.

The disciples in the boat during the storm at night stand for the Christians in their unbelief and fear. John has included the story, taking it from the tradition, but he has not apparently made much of it. Perhaps he retained it because in it Jesus says It is I, which is literally I AM, just as in the I AM sayings. If they reflect on who Jesus is, as John will in the discourse that follows, they need not be afraid any more.

Like Nicodemus earlier in the gospel, the people address Jesus as Rabbi, and like him they are stating their unbelief in him, because they are asking how he had crossed the lake; they are still at a level that is confused and questioning, they have not yet seen what the sign signifies. As in the case of the Samaritan woman, the discussion involves misunderstanding and irony: they ask Jesus to give them the bread, which is himself, without realizing that they can only have it through having faith in him; they ask for a sign to authenticate faith, without realizing that the sign has already been given to them, in the miracle of the loaves. They perceive that Jesus is claiming to replace Moses, so their question is, What is the evidence to support and validate such a claim?

Jesus is both giver and gift, and those who believe in him receive, by their union with him in faith, the life that is union with God. But once again the point is made that faith is not an option but a gift, an effect: believers are the present which the Father gives to the Son, in order that the Son may give them life. This life is available now and will continue forever; the future, the last day, cannot add to what is given now, since the gift is always the same: it is union with the same Jesus, the bread of life.

To those who are not believers, what Jesus is saying seems extraordinary and ridiculous. They complain, much as the Israelites in the wilderness complained at the time when God gave them manna. Jesus surpasses the manna because those who receive him will never die.

John uses language that seems to recall the eucharist, and the passage has often been understood as if it were meant to be a substitute for the institution of the supper on the night of the betrayal; yet it need not be read in that way. To eat a person's flesh, in the Old Testament, is to be his destroyer, and to drink someone's blood is to take responsibility for his life, as David refused to do when he poured out the water drawn for him from the well at Bethlehem. Jesus relates himself to those who believe in him as food to those who eat it; for food to fulfil its purpose, it must be destroyed by the eater: for Jesus to be the life-giver, he must die.

The requirement that the saviour must die offends the disciples because it threatens their false belief in their independence of God and their ability to save themselves. They need both his death and his exaltation, and the gift of the Spirit, before they can believe and understand.

Once more we notice John's insistence that faith is a gift, not an option that is open to anyone to take of his own volition. This implies a belief in election; John held that some were chosen by God to be believers. Yet even to be chosen by Jesus to be one of the twelve was not a guarantee of salvation, as the inclusion of Judas Iscariot showed.

John thought that salvation was too important to be left to us; he felt a strong attraction for the idea that everything is in the hands of God. Sometimes he writes as though human freedom had no reality; but that would be to make nonsense of his perception of God's love for his creatures and will to save them without destroying their status as persons. Like others before and after him, he wants to say both that everything is in God's control, and that we are free to choose.

7.1–8.59 (omitting 7.53–8.11) I am the light of the world

In this section of his gospel, John sets out various degrees of faith, from sheer unbelief, through varieties of partial faith, to that kind of faith in Jesus that John wants his readers to share with him. The nature of faith is the link between this part of the book and the discourse after the feeding of the five thousand that immediately precedes it. The brothers of Jesus who, like his mother, are not given their names in this gospel, represent unbelief, and so do groups variously referred to as the Pharisees, the chief priests and the Jews. But there are others, the crowd for example and the officers, who raise the question whether Jesus is the Christ and believe on account of the signs. Jesus declares who he is and what should be believed, but this leads only to an attempt to destroy him by stoning.

The distribution of rôles among the various groups in the narrative is a device of the author's and helps to clarify the nature of faith, but has no historical value; the Pharisees, for example, act in a way that is impossible historically, as though they had some administrative or judicial authority alongside the chief priests.

The unifying theme of the section is not set out at the beginning by means of signs, as John has done previously; here he varies his method, and the theme is provided in the statement that it was the feast of Tabernacles in Jerusalem. This festival was held in the autumn, and was originally associated with vine-harvest and prayers for rain; part of the celebration was the illumination of the court of the women in the temple with lamps. This provides the context for John's second I AM saying:

Jesus, not the Law and not the Temple, is the light of the world; to live in union with him through faith is to be in the light; that is, to be delivered from ignorance, sin and death.

Those who do not believe in Jesus are not neutral; unbelief, as John sees it, is not simply the absence of faith, but a destructive force which expresses itself as hatred of Jesus and the desire to do away with him. Jesus is the prime evidence that unbelief is wrong, so those who do not believe want to destroy him. This rôle is played out by the Jews, here and throughout this gospel; they are the representatives and spokesmen of the world, that is, of all those who live as though there were no God. Here too John is using dramatic licence; all the first Christians were in fact Jews, but John writes as though there had never been any Jewish Christian communities.

The brothers of Jesus also are represented as though they were unbelievers, whereas in fact they held leading positions in the Jerusalem church; they speak in the gospel as though their only motivation were success, and the more of it the better. They do not see that there is any problem in Jesus showing himself to the world, whereas John knows that the reaction of the world to such a revelation must be determination to destroy the revealer. This will indeed be the eventual outcome, but it must happen at the right time, the time which is in God's hand, and that is not yet. Jesus says to them that he will not go to the feast and then he goes.

This is the third instance of the johannine device in which a suggestion is made to Jesus which he rejects, but later agrees to. John's purpose in using it may be to demonstrate that Jesus does not act in obedience to human requests, even to those of his mother and his brothers, but only in obedience to the Father's will.

That Jesus is unusual becomes apparent to the Jews when he teaches in the temple; his teaching is not the result of study, but is what the Father has told him to say, and that is that he is the one sent by God, the one who is to be believed, the one who gives life to those who believe in him. There is, in this gospel, no other teaching of Jesus than this. The only thing that Jesus says is that he is the agent of God. God's will is that Jesus should be believed, therefore anyone who wants to do God's will will recognize Jesus as the one whom God has sent and not as an imposter.

Jesus accuses the Jews of wanting to kill him, and this recalls what John had said about the previous visit to Jerusalem, that they wanted to kill him because of the signs that he did, particularly healing on the sabbath. Jesus points out that the healing of the lame man was a greater thing than circumcision, yet that was permitted on the sabbath.

With great irony it is then suggested that an objection to faith in Jesus as the Christ is that the origin of Jesus is known; his father was Joseph. This supposed difficulty is, of course, unreal, since the origin of Jesus is God the Father, whom they do not know, for had they known the Father, they would have known the Son also. In contrast with this unbelief which is ascribed to the authorities in the temple, John places an imperfect faith that he attributes to many in the crowd; its inferiority to genuine faith is indicated by the statement that it is based on the signs that Jesus has performed, understood as miracles and wonders but nothing more.

Jesus then speaks in riddles of going away, being sought but not found, and of his inaccessibility, but these riddles are not understood by the crowd or by the authorities. The reader, however, knows what is meant and understands that Jesus is referring to his exaltation upon the cross to the glory that he had with the Father before he came into the world. The Jews think he is talking about a mission to the hellenistic world. What John has done here is to have tried to help the insider to understand what the outsider makes of the language of faith. Expressions that are clear in their meaning to one group mean something entirely different to the other. John wants his readers to be aware of the gulf between faith and unbelief.

The meaning of the utterance of Jesus on the last day of the feast is uncertain, because we cannot be sure how John intended the sentence to be punctuated. (At the time when John wrote, and for many years after, there was no punctuation in Greek manuscripts; there were not even spaces between the words.) If we follow the RSV margin and the NEB text, Jesus says that he is the giver of real water to those who are thirsty and thus the giver of real life to those who long for something better than the life that is available here, apart from Christ. Jesus is the fountain from which this water comes, because he will give the Spirit to the believers when he has been lifted up, both on the cross and in the resurrection.

After this, John shows yet again the inadequacy of the previous Christian understanding of Jesus, as a prophet, the Son of David, or the man born at Bethlehem. This way of placing Jesus in a prepared category will not do, John means; scripture predicted Jesus, he believes, but he exceeds expectation. The event is greater than the forecast.

The officers who had been sent to arrest Jesus now bear witness to him and say that he speaks as no man has ever spoken before; to John this is indeed the truth, but the Pharisees think that the officers have been deceived and they appeal to authority. Nicodemus asks for a more open attitude, but he is rebuked by the others as a fellow-Galilean, as though one would only raise the possibility of Jesus being genuinely what he said he was if one had some hidden and irrelevant reason for doing so, such as having been born in the same district. The poverty of the arguments against faith demonstrates the weakness of the position of those who deploy them.

The reader of John's gospel should pass straight from 7.52 to 8.12, omitting the intervening paragraph which in some editions of the New Testament is printed here as part of the text; in other editions it is put at the bottom of the page or at the end of the gospel. It is now generally accepted that the story of Jesus and the adulterous woman, though it is part of scripture, is not part of John's book. Some of the most reliable manuscripts of John do not have it at all, and others have it in a different position in the New Testament. The reason why someone copying John's book inserted it here may be because it illustrates the saying of Jesus in the next paragraph, I judge no one.

To return to the gospel, the position John wants to establish with regard to faith in Jesus is that he is the unique and final agent of God, his only Son. This faith, as John sees it, has two aspects, one negative and the other positive: the positive aspect is that through Jesus everything that is needed for salvation is available; the negative is that Jesus is nothing in himself, but only the agent of the Father, the one through whom the Father works. Jesus is thus both everything and nothing, simultaneously. These two aspects of what is to be believed about Jesus become the subject of the discussion between him and the Jews in the remaining part of this section of the gospel.

Thus the second I AM saying promises light and life to the follower of Jesus, and is an example of the positive aspect of what is to be believed about him; similarly the claim of Jesus to know his origin and destiny also places him in a unique relation to the Father, as does his claim to have authority to bear witness to himself, and to judge. But these activities are all grounded in his obedience to the Father and his dependence on him, and it is this that is the cause of unbelief. Unbelief is an attempt to live without God, as though he did not exist and as though the world and its inhabitants were not his creatures. The practical atheism by which many of us live makes it impossible to believe in the Son whose existence is his dependence upon the Father.

Where is your Father? is thus the essential problem for unbelief, and the answer to the question can only be, You know neither me nor my Father. A world that despises dependence and prizes power and glory above everything else cannot believe in one whose only authorization is his total submission to another. If they knew what they were, they would understand who he was; but since they cannot, or do not, understand themselves, they do not and cannot understand him.

Once again Jesus speaks ambiguously of going away, meaning that he will die and be exalted to God, but this is misunderstood as though he meant that he would commit suicide. Their lack of understanding shows that they belong to a different world from him, a world of darkness and evil, from which only faith in him can rescue them. There is hope, however; their unbelief will be the cause of his death; and his death and resurrection will demonstrate his dependence on the Father; through this, he promises, they will come to know who he is. John often seems pessimistic about the possibility of faith overcoming unbelief, but here he states the opposite point of view: the enemies of Jesus will know who he is; unbelief will be routed by faith, and darkness by light. So the claim to be the light of the world should not be understood as an offer of salvation only to those who follow, but as a promise to everyone: the darkness will be overcome by the light; Jesus is the light of the world, not only of the elect. We may remember the words of John's prologue: The light shines in the darkness and the darkness cannot put it out.

As a foretaste of this, John says that many believed on him; but then he shows that this belief was only a foretaste and sign of what true faith will be, by disclosing the inadequacy of this faith of the Jews. The Jews who believe suppose that they are free because they are members of God's people Israel; but to John this is not so; there must be a total break with the past, a re-birth, and faith in Jesus such that one sees the scriptures, Moses, the Temple and the Law as signs, and only as signs, of the reality that has only now come into the world.

In what sense does John think that the Jews are not free? In his book they speak for unbelief and are the representatives of the world. Seen in this way their sin is the rejection of their creator, and they demonstrate their sin by their desire to destroy Jesus and thus eliminate the final evidence for the existence of God. They do this, without knowing what they are doing, but thinking that they are God's people, the descendents of Abraham; religion conceals reality from the religious. To claim to have some status in relation to God through Abraham is to attach oneself to something other than Christ, and to mistake the sign for the reality; as John understands it, this is not just a regrettable mistake, but demonic: it is to become a child of the devil and to follow him in murder. Their intention to kill Jesus shows that this is so.

Unbelief is devilish; it twists us into living a life that cannot be sustained because it flies in the face of the facts. The truth is that God is God and we are not; the lie is that if we disobey him we shall be as God. To believe in the lie makes it impossible to believe in Christ, who has come as the truth, and lives it out, and dies to prove it.

The section ends with the conclusion that Jesus is greater than Abraham, and that he is the giver of the life that never dies; yet he is also nothing, because he is dependent on the Father. The Father glorifies him, he does not glorify himself. Indeed he is greater than Abraham, because he is God's Word through whom everything came into existence. This assertion of his divinity acts as a further incentive to destroy him, in the minds of those who do not believe that they are creatures.

9.1–10.21   *I am the light, the door and the shepherd*

In the previous section John has shown us the bitter conflict that exists between the representatives of the religious establishment and Jesus the light of the world. They want to destroy him, because they stand for and are part of a system that is closed and complete; it has coped with all problems, including God. For them there are no unanswered questions, but the law provides them with solutions, and the temple represents a religion that is satisfying and apparently fulfilling. They are like Job's comforters in the Old Testament who think they can explain the mystery of God, and just as they roused God's wrath, so Jesus is totally opposed to the Jewish leaders.

This conflict is the background of another sign: in the story, it is the conflict between Jesus and the Pharisees, but the evangelist means it to be understood as the condemnation of all who think that God's way can be contained within religious provisions. Just as the Jews had tried to stone Jesus, now they attempt to do away with the evidence given in the sign, by casting doubt upon the truth of the witnesses. John makes it clear that unbelief will go to any length to destroy faith and the grounds for faith; though it is faced with an impossible task, it pursues it relentlessly: the task is to stop people from believing in God. History shows that faith keeps on breaking out; it is irrepressible.

The sign that John records here is the one that exactly fits the theme of this section of his book: Jesus gives sight to a man who had been born blind. The man's congenital blindness stands for both the ignorance of the leaders of religious institutions and more generally for the inadequacy of life as it is here and now. We are all born blind, John means, and need a miracle in order to be able to see things as they really are; that is, to believe in God. So though the sign acts as a criticism of Judaism and of any other religion that claims to give a complete answer to the problems of life, it also provides hope because the gift of Jesus is seen to make it possible to have faith in the God who really is. This is why Jesus reveals himself in the discourses that follow as the door by which we come to God, and as the shepherd who protects his sheep and gives them life.

Notice how John indicates the end of the section by returning to its beginning, with the question, Can a demon open the eyes of the blind? This is just one very small example of the skill which John uses in writing this section of the book; every word plays an important part, none is wasted.

There were accounts of the healing of blind men in Mark's gospel, and John is probably using those or similar traditions; but he has developed the simpler story such as we find in the earlier gospels into a much longer narrative, in order to express the faith in Jesus that he wants his readers to share.

If sickness was a punishment for sin, as some believed, then who had sinned when a child was born blind? Jesus directs the disciples away from the theoretical question to the practical issue: the man who had been born blind is an opportunity for revealing God's works, that is, his power to overcome darkness and ignorance and unbelief by the gift of faith and understanding.

This rejection of theory in favour of practice is typical of John's enterprise, and is an aspect of his overall intention to replace doctrine with the personal relationship with Jesus.

The time for Jesus to do these works is limited, because he will not always be with them in the flesh; it is therefore appropriate that he should seize this opportunity and cure this man's blindness. Elisha had cured a man of leprosy through commanding him to wash in the Jordan; Jesus sends the blind man to the pool called Siloam (meaning Sent), and its name is significant because it points to Jesus, the one who has been sent into the world by the Father.

Once the cure is complete, the argument begins; and, at each of its stages, there is always a group of characters ready to take up the position of unbelief, dismissal and destruction. First, it is the turn of those who had known the man in the past; some of them say that this person who can see is a different person, so there has been no miracle. The man says to them It is I, using the same expression in Greek that is translated I AM when Jesus speaks it. The gift of sight has changed the man into a witness, and we shall see how his faith develops as the story proceeds. But throughout the story, his faith is built upon facts that to him are irrefutable; and the first of these is that he is the man who used to be a beggar, and not anybody else. They then ask him to explain how the change from blindness to sight has come about, and the man replies in the most matter-of-fact and value-free manner in which he can; he refers to a man called Jesus, repeats what he did and said and what he himself did, and says what the result was. The enquiry cannot go any further at this stage, because the man is confining himself to facts as he knows them and cannot therefore answer the question where Jesus is; his faith is not yet able to express itself in the belief that Jesus is in the Father, and that he acts in obedience to him.

It is only when the man is brought before the Pharisees (again presented by John as though they formed some kind of judicial court) that his faith grows and develops into the belief that Jesus is from God; their opposition and questioning have the effect of enabling his faith to mature, and their exclusion of him from Judaism will be the prelude to his final statement of belief. That is to say, their destructiveness is unintentionally constructive, because evil plays into the hands of good, and the devil does God's work for him without meaning to. All this will become clear in John's account of the crucifixion.

The statement that the healing took place on the sabbath, when it would be contrary to the law to make clay and anoint eyes, adds a further element to the situation. The Pharisees can now appeal to the law and condemn Jesus for disobedience to the will of God as it was revealed there. The opposite side of the case is stated by others: how did the miracle happen, how did God intervene and remove the man's blindness if Jesus, the one through whom the cure took place, was breaking God's law? The fact of the division between those who dismiss Jesus as a sabbath-breaker and those who wonder why God acted at his request can only point in one direction; but it is a direction in which none of the Pharisees could go without ceasing to be Pharisees: it would be necessary to say that Jesus was greater than Moses and the law, and that the time of fulfilment had come. Rather than take this step they ask the man what his solution to the problem is, and at this stage in the development of his faith he adopts the inadequate confession, as John wants us to see it, that Jesus is a prophet. We know that this is only a temporary solution, and unsatisfactory; it does not explain all the facts; prophets do not act contrary to the law.

The desperate ingenuity with which unbelief finds ways of avoiding the plain sense of the evidence before its eyes is now illustrated by the Jews, who send for the parents of the man, hoping to find an alternative explanation of the apparent miracle. But the parents, like their son, stick to the facts: they are the parents of the man; he was born blind; he does now see. They refuse to go any further than that, for fear of the reprisals that the Jews would take in excluding them from the synagogue. So they hand the discussion back to the man on whom the miracle was performed.

At his second appearance before them, the Pharisees have adopted one of the two positions held during their previous enquiry; they assume that Jesus is a law-breaker. This enables the man to offer the damaging criticism of their position, by re-asserting the fact of the cure. He can be sure of that; it is the only thing that is certain, as far as he is concerned. In their despair of ever finding a non-miraculous solution they ask him to tell them again what happened, and at this point the man sees through their bluster and begins to mock them: Do they want him to convert them to faith by re-telling the story of his healing? This makes them harden their position; they appeal to authority, the law, the unchanging will of God. They can be certain of that, but not about the origin of Jesus who may be from the devil and acting with his power. The mention of this possibility deepens the faith and understanding of the man whose sight Jesus has restored; in his unsophisticated simplicity he can distinguish sinners from worshippers of God, good men from bad. He believes in a God who answers the prayers of the righteous; and he has lived until now with the knowledge that there is no cure for congenital blindness. So he progresses to a more developed faith, that Jesus must be from God, and not, as they say, a sinner. They now take up the position mentioned by the disciples at the beginning of the story, and say that the man's blindness points to his sinful origin: he is himself a sinner and has been from birth, and his blindness proves it. Thus unbelief leads to moral judgements, both on Jesus and on the man who was cured and became a witness; this is its way of discrediting evidence that points to faith.

In the final paragraph of the story Jesus, who has been absent from the scene since the miracle, returns and speaks to the man, revealing the reversal of rôles which is the result of his coming into the world: the blind see, and those who think they see become blind. It may be that we have here another allusion to the story of Elisha and the leper, because there the leprosy of Naaman is transferred to Gehazi (2 Kings 5).

The climax of the story is the judgement which is an inevitable result of the coming of Jesus; God's revelation creates either faith or unbelief.

The allegory of the sheepfold, the door and the shepherd follows immediately and draws out certain points from the sign. There is first the contrast between thieves and the shepherd, who correspond to the Pharisees and Jesus respectively. Jesus is both the one who enters by the door and the door through which the shepherd enters. The sheep can distinguish thieves from shepherd; they are not deceived by false religious leaders who are self-serving. This is the criterion by which a shepherd is to be known: does he lay down his life for the sheep? Thieves, robbers and those who are paid to work have no interest in the sheep but only in what they can gain for themselves from them. The owner's interest is in the well-being of his sheep; theirs is not.

It is clear that John's allegory is not a parable, and that the meaning of the picture has affected the way in which it is drawn. Shepherds in fact keep sheep in order to make a profit; they live off their sheep. Already in the Old Testament, however, the language of shepherds and sheep had been used of those who have authority over others, whether as kings or as other religious leaders.

Jesus is the one who surrenders his life in order that others may live. John had made the same point through the metaphor of eating; we live by his destruction. Now he makes it through the figure of the shepherd, recalling how David, in the Old Testament, risked his life in fighting lions and bears when he kept his father's sheep (1 Samuel 17). Jesus' devotion to his own exceeds this because it involves his death.

We can either dismiss what Jesus claims for himself as madness, or we can postpone a decision. These are the alternatives stated by John at the end of the section. Against the explanation that Jesus is mad and possessed by a demon is the fact that demons do not heal people who are blind; so the charge of black-magic will not stick. We are left to wonder what should be believed about Jesus, and what sort of faith in him would be appropriate.

10.22–42 Jesus and the Father

The answer to the question, Who is Jesus? is now given; it is given to the Jews in Jerusalem, in the temple, during the Feast of Dedication, in Solomon's portico. Each of the details is recorded because of its significance: Jesus is the bringer of salvation which, as John has already said, is of the Jews; they are his own people, and his body is the true temple, because he is the one whom the Father consecrated. He is the Son of God who does the works of God, just as Solomon the son of David did the works prepared for him by his father in building the first temple on this site.

The Jews complain that Jesus does not tell them plainly who he is; but we know that this is not the real problem; we can be told things and yet not hear what is said to us, because we are not ready or willing to receive it. The fault here lies with the Jews, not with Jesus. And yet, John insists in his characteristic manner, it is not their fault, because faith is not simply a choice that anyone is free to make. Only those who are chosen can believe; only those whom the Father has given to the Son can hear when Jesus says who he is. John's explanation worries us, but he knew no better way to account for the fact that there were believers, and unbelievers too.

The Father, John says, has given some to Jesus, to believe and be saved; Jesus will give them eternal life and they will never lose it; the will of the Father and the will of the Son are identical, they both will the salvation of the elect.

This seems blasphemy to the Jews and provokes a further attempt on the life of Jesus. He explains that he is not, as they suppose, making himself God; it is God who has resolved that all those who believe in him should share his life, and he has revealed this in scripture; if believers share in the life of God, how much more does Jesus himself, the one through whom God has shown himself to the world as the giver of life? The answer to the question, Who is Jesus? is thus: that he is the Son of God and that he does what his Father does. Faith in such a Son of God will be difficult for those who have always and rightly maintained the unity of God in a world of many gods; but at least they should not deny that what Jesus is doing is the work of God. To think of him as demonic and in league with Satan is to contradict the plain sense of the facts. However difficult it may be to find appropriate ways of speaking about Jesus, it is important that they retain the facts and reflect on them: Jesus is on the side of God, and what he does is what God does; he brings light and life and healing to those who are sick and dying and blind.

We may not be responsible for our faith, because faith is a gift, and because it goes beyond the facts; but we are responsible for the account we give of the facts. The man who had been cured of his blindness gave a scrupulously exact account of how the cure took place; a similar attention to what is the case is required in the things of Jesus. Paul had used the same argument with the Galatians; there was, he said, only one question that needed to be asked: In what way did they receive the Spirit; by works or by faith? Here too in John's gospel everything depends on seeing clearly and not letting prejudice control what is thought to be going on.

The return of Jesus to the place whence, in one sense, he had come, that is, the place where John baptized and bore witness to Jesus, provides a space in the narrative before the account of the final sign. John had borne witness to Jesus as one who was greater; John had not done any miraculous signs; Jesus has done them and through these signs many have come to believe. There will be one more sign and it will have a two-fold effect: it will point to the truth that Jesus is the life, and it will be the cause of his death.

11.1–54 *I am the resurrection*

From the very beginning of his gospel John has described Jesus as both light and life; these are two of the symbols he uses most frequently. He gave us a sign that pointed to Jesus as light, in the healing of the man born blind; now, in his final sign, the theme will be that Jesus is life. The story of the raising of Lazarus will be followed immediately, and as the direct result of the miracle, by the decision of the council to put Jesus to death. This sequence of events will come as no surprise to the reader of the book; he has already been led to see that unbelief is destructive, and that it is under internal compulsion to destroy the evidence that is against it. As Jesus has disclosed more and more of what it is he has come to do, the opposition has become more and more determined to do away with him. The giving of life is the cause of his death. But a further layer of meaning can also be seen: John has made it abundantly clear, again and again, that the whole story of Jesus is within the control of God; his actions are done in obedience to the Father; his movements depend upon the observance of the hour; he is totally dependent upon the one who sent him and completely focused on him. So what human beings do when they decide to put Jesus to death is only an effect on the surface of events; deeper down is the will of the Father and the obedience of the Son. Human initiatives and plans play into the divine purpose and bring it to completion. Dying is the way in which Jesus gives his life to others.

The relation between this sign in John's gospel and similar material in the other gospels is complicated and confusing. To begin with, there is no account of the restoration to life of a man called Lazarus in any gospel other than this one; nor is there any account in the other gospels of a miracle of restoration to life in or near Jerusalem shortly before the crucifixion. The other evangelists do indeed include stories of the raising of the dead, but not at this point in the narrative; and their stories are very different from this one. Secondly, Martha and her sister Mary are mentioned in Luke's gospel, but they are not said there to have had a brother called Lazarus; Lazarus, however, is the name of a character in a parable of Jesus in Luke's gospel; and the possibility of the return of this Lazarus from the dead is discussed there by Abraham and the rich man. Thirdly, the other three evangelists suggest or imply that the immediate cause of the decision of the Jews to proceed against Jesus was the entry into Jerusalem, or the cleansing of the temple, or the parable of the vineyard; but in John the cleansing of the temple comes at the beginning of the book, and the parable of the vineyard is not included, any more than any of the parables, and the entry into Jerusalem follows, rather than precedes, the decision to do away with Jesus.

Whatever solution we adopt to the question of the historicity of this miracle, we can see that from the point of view of the symbolism that is being used, the themes in the gospel, the development of the story, the exposition of theology and the explanation of faith, John's final sign had to be a miracle of raising the dead. The last enemy is death, and the last sign must be the sign that points to life. As in the case of the first sign, turning water into wine, the story may have been created by faith, to express faith.

The message that the sisters send to Jesus is an implied request that he should come and heal Lazarus so that he will not die. We have already seen how such requests are dealt with in this gospel: at first Jesus refuses to act, but later he does what he was asked to do, and what he does exceeds the expectations of those who asked. His works and his time are in the Father's hands; he can only do what the Father commands him to do. His statement is a typically johannine riddle which can be understood in different ways; in fact it must be understood in various ways, because on one level it is simply not true. The illness of Lazarus will in fact lead to his death and burial, but is will also lead to his restoration to life in the flesh, which is a sign pointing to eternal life; it is not more than a sign, it is not the gift itself, since, as we shall see, the Jews will plan to put Lazarus to death: he is vulnerable, and will in any case die again some day. Jesus performs the sign and raises Lazarus, and in this way he reveals the glory of God which is to give eternal life to human beings and share his existence with them; but he is also providing the occasion that will lead to his own death. And this is not all, because, as John will make abundantly clear, Jesus glorifies God by his death, and is himself glorified by being lifted up on the cross. Thus the statement of Jesus at the beginning of the story causes us to reflect upon the death and life of Lazarus, the death and glory of Jesus which will follow, and the revelation of the glory of God; and these are all elements within the story as John will tell it.

Jesus delays and does not go to Bethany, and at this point in the narrative this is inexplicable. But one possible explanation is ruled out; it is not because Jesus does not love the two sisters and their brother; John assures us that he does. The reason for the delay must therefore be sought elsewhere; the whole story must be read as more than the performance of an act of kindness and affection. It will be a sign, it will point to something else, and it will do this more effectively by containing contradictions and ambiguities at the narrative level. We might compare an incident in Mark's gospel where Jesus is presented as looking for figs at a time when they were not in season, as Mark specifically says; and this is in order to direct our attention to what the story symbolizes, which is God's expectation that his people will pay him the good works that he has commanded them to render.

Once the time to delay is over, Jesus invites the disciples to accompany him from the place where they are on the east side of the Jordan into Judaea to the home of Lazarus; but they express surprise, which is based on their unbelief: they address him as Rabbi, always a bad omen; they think that the Jews can destroy Jesus, but they should know that he is in God's hands; they imagine that his death will be by stoning, but we shall see that he will be raised up on the cross. Jesus answers their unbelief parabolically: he is the light of the world, therefore there cannot be any accident or misadventure when he is present; divine control is paramount.

John's intention in telling the story of Lazarus is to enable the reader to believe in Jesus as the resurrection, and he does this by using words that have more than one meaning. Moreover, we are helped to catch John's intended meaning by seeing how the characters in the story misunderstand what is being said. Almost everything that is spoken by the minor characters is a misunderstanding, and when we realize that, it is then possible to see what John wants us to understand. Mistakes, when they are recognized as mistakes, serve to express the truth. A good example of this procedure is provided immediately, when Jesus says that Lazarus has fallen asleep, and the disciples take this in the literal sense, whereas what was intended was a reference to his death. This is carefully explained to the reader, in order that once he has picked up the method he can apply it himself as the story continues and ambiguities and misunderstandings occur again and again.

We are now shown why Jesus delayed and did not set out for Bethany as soon as the message reached him from the sisters. He will only act in the way that will provide faith for his disciples, and he could not have done this had not Lazarus died; it is implied that Lazarus would not have died if Jesus had gone immediately he heard of his sickness. Thomas' comment to the other disciples expresses unbelief: he expects to die with Lazarus, or with Jesus (who is going to the place where the Jews are seeking his life) – it is not clear which. But both expectations are wrong: Lazarus will live, and Thomas cannot yet die with Jesus, any more than Peter can follow Jesus to his death; Jesus must die for his disciples to make it possible for them to be martyrs. So, Let us also go, that we may die with him, can be understood in different ways, and all of them will be untrue.

This is the last we hear of the disciples in this story; they have expressed a blindness that needs no further description. From now on, there are only two groups of characters, apart from Jesus himself; they take the centre of the stage: they are the sisters, and the Jews. The sisters have an imperfect and inadequate faith which is too closely involved with the performance of miracles and the expectation of the resurrection on the last day; the Jews have faith in Jesus only as a prophet, but mainly, as elsewhere in John, they stand for unbelief.

John presents the two sisters as different characters, and this may recall the contrast in Luke's gospel between Mary who sat at Jesus' feet and Martha who attended to the meal. Here too it is

Martha who goes out to meet Jesus, but Mary sits in the house; and this distinction between the sisters makes it possible for John to repeat the conversation between the women and Jesus and by this repetition to make the point that he wants made more emphatically.

Martha rebukes Jesus for not coming sooner, and for not healing Lazarus; but she makes a further statement, that defines Jesus as one who asks God for gifts. The suggestion is therefore that she is asking for Lazarus to be raised to life, like the daughter of Jairus or the son of the widow in the other gospels; but though this is what will happen, it will not be the whole point of telling the story, and if Martha cannot see more than that Jesus is in a position to ask God to perform miracles through him, even the ultimate miracle of raising the dead, she will not have seen what John believes most passionately, and what it is that his book is written to convey. Jesus says that Lazarus will rise, and Martha understands this to refer to the general resurrection at the last day, a faith that would be shared by Pharisees, for example. Neither that, nor the miracle that is about to happen, is what John's sign points to. The I AM saying is the key; Jesus is the resurrection, in the sense that he gives life to those who believe in him, and this life is not affected by physical death, because it is eternal. Martha does not yet believe this, and her answer shows that this is so; she is still talking in terms of a future coming into the world, that is, she is still putting Jesus into a Jewish way of thinking. The reality is greater than the expectation, and than the sign that points to it. The reality is that the believers never die, because they are united with the one who is the resurrection, now and forever; death cannot separate them from him.

We are shown Martha's inadequate faith again, when she refers to Jesus as Teacher, a title that does not at all express what John believes about Jesus. The Jews similarly, and to an even greater extent, speak as people who are wrong, mistaken, in the dark. They suppose that Mary is going to the tomb to weep for her dead brother, but we know that she is going to meet the one who is the resurrection. She too rebukes Jesus for his delay in coming to Bethany, exactly as Martha had done, and she weeps, putting herself into the same group as the Jews, who are also weeping. This causes deep emotion in Jesus, and it is the emotion of anger in the face of unbelief. His question is intended as the prelude to the sign, but they think that he also means to weep at the dead man's grave. Here, and in the only other place in the gospels where it is said that Jesus wept, the cause is wrath at the blindness and stupidity of human beings. The Jews do not understand him in this way, so they look around for other explanations: it must be because Jesus loved Lazarus. We know that that was not the reason for his tears; he would not have stayed two days beyond the Jordan and set out only when he knew that Lazarus was dead, if when he came he was over-whelmed with grief. Nor is the other explanation any better: he could indeed have stopped Lazarus from dying, just as he had given life to the official's son at Capernaum when he was at the point of death. The Jews cannot know the cause of his tears, because the cause of his tears is their ignorance, of which they are unaware.

Martha continues to speak from the point of view of an inadequate faith, warning Jesus of the stench of a corpse that has been dead four days, and Jesus rebukes her. His relationship with the Father is revealed in his prayer, in which he declares the union that always exists between them. The Son has complete confidence in his communion with the Father, and only speaks aloud in order that others may believe in his mission from God and share the eternal life of the Father and the Son. Then, as he had predicted, the dead man hears the voice of the Son of God and comes out. But this is not the general resurrection at the last day; Lazarus is still flesh and blood as the bandages and cloth reveal; he must be untied; whereas, at the final resurrection, the mortal will put on immortality. This is a sign of the resurrec-tion, and a sign that operates in a particular way: it points to the continuing life of Lazarus while he is the tomb. Those who believe in Jesus never die; Lazarus is called out, as though he were simply asleep; John does not say here that Jesus raised him from the dead. The sign points to that eternal life which is given in and with faith, and does not have to be waited for, to be received only in an age to come.

There is a direct link of cause and effect between this sign and the decision of the Jewish council to destroy Jesus. The Jews see that his signs lead to faith; and faith in Jesus, they also see, will lead to the destruction of the temple and of the Jewish nation; and this is a true perception, in that types and shadows have their ending. Unbelief must protect itself (there is no one else to protect it) and destroy what threatens it; and this is the insight of the high priest. He prophesies without meaning to do so; he declares the law that the minority must give way to the majority; but he does not see that what will happen will be that one will die on behalf of others, both Jews and Gentiles. The high priest's prophecy, which John explains to his reader, is one example of a device that John will use again, in the account of the trial of Jesus, when Pilate also will say more than he intends and become a witness to the truth without realizing it.

The decision has been taken to put Jesus to death, but the time for it has not yet come, so the hour must be awaited. Jesus and the disciples withdraw to the country near the wilderness until God's moment arrives.

11.55–12.36a *Preparations for the Passover*

All four evangelists, and Paul too, associate the death of Jesus with the Passover festival, the annual Jewish celebration of the Exodus of the Israelites from Egypt under the leadership of Moses. In John, Jesus' death takes place on the afternoon before the evening when the Passover meal will be eaten, and just as John had contrasted Jesus with Moses, Jacob, the law, the temple, circumcision and the feast of Tabernacles, so now he will use the Passover festival in such a way as to contrast the Jewish celebration that is going on at the time with the real and final gift of God that Jesus is making available by his death and exaltation. Thus at the beginning of this section the feast is referred to as the Passover of the Jews, and that qualifying expression, Of the Jews, presents the occasion in a particular way in this gospel, as an event that belongs only to the past, the time of preparation and prophecy, and of all that is superseded and set aside by the coming of Jesus. According to John's way of writing, the Jews are those who are without faith and blind. They come to purify themselves in order to keep the feast, but we know that they will in fact take part in the destruction of Jesus who is the true lamb of God. They do not know what they are doing. They look for him and discuss whether he will come, but they have no knowledge because they have no faith; their questions remain unanswered as far as they are concerned. Their leaders on the other hand have taken their decision and laid plans for the arrest of Jesus.

The situation is this: the Jews are preparing for a festival that is to be made redundant through the arrival of its fulfilment; they are purifying themselves for this; but simultaneously their leaders are preparing to arrest and kill Jesus; his death will be the true Passover, in which release from sin and freedom to live will be made available for those who believe. The irony of the situation lies in the mistaken action of the Jews, which is self-destruction; their piety is blind and will effect the end they had not intended. They are wondering whether Jesus will come to the feast as a fellow-participant; we know that he will come and be the lamb.

John tells the story of the anointing, but with different emphases from the other evangelists. Lazarus, whose living presence is a reminder of who Jesus is, eats with Jesus; Martha serves, as in Luke, and Mary anoints the feet of Jesus, like an unnamed woman also in Luke; Judas is the disciple who objects to the use of the ointment, and his reason for objecting is supplied; it is because he is a thief. Jesus speaks of his burial, and of the time when he will no longer be present in the flesh to be anointed. It is a story of conflict between the woman who gives and the man who wants to get, and Jesus is on the side of the woman. Of course John knows that the believer is a receiver and that he is entirely dependent on God for grace and life. But the act by which one receives can be thought of as a kind of giving rather than getting; faith is self-surrender, offering, oblation. Mary's action is symbolic of faith, and Judas, one of the twelve, is her opposite.

John returns once again to the inadequacy of faith that is grounded on miracles, and to the destructiveness of unbelief, two of his favourite topics. To want to see Lazarus is a mistaken and superficial motive, when Jesus, the resurrection, is present; to attend to the sign, when the reality to which it points is there also, is to misunderstand both; the sign should be left behind because it has fulfilled its function. The leaders of Judaism think they must now destroy Lazarus, because his existence is leading people into this half-faith in Jesus. Their previous decision to kill Jesus requires them to make other similar decisions in order to pursue their policy consistently; and the plan to eliminate Lazarus demonstrates the evil of their whole enterprise, since there is no conceivable reason why he should die, except that he is inconvenient to their cause.

John re-tells the story of the entry into Jerusalem in his own way. In the other gospels, Jesus sends for the ass and rides on it, and the people respond with their greetings; in John, the welcome of the people comes first, and the riding on the ass follows. Jesus is welcomed as King of Israel by those who believe because of the raising of Lazarus, and they bear witness; what they do not understand, what makes their faith imperfect, is that Jesus will not be made king by them, or by the use of force; he is to be exalted by laying down his life. This re-arrangement of the order of events so that the fulfilment of the prophecy follows the greeting of the crowd shows that his way of being king will be different from what they expect. The irony of the situation is drawn out by the Pharisees who speak the truth in a way they do not mean, and say that they cannot come out of this situation with any advantage; but the world has become *his* followers. There is both truth and error in what they say: error, in that the crowd does not yet believe; and truth, in that it does so partially, as we are shown in the Greeks who have come to Jerusalem to worship at Passover and want to see Jesus.

Their request is brought to Jesus by disciples whose names are Greek, not Aramaic; and it elicits from Jesus the statement that the hour has come. This announcement puts a bracket round all that has happened so far, from the sign at Cana when Jesus first mentioned his hour, to this point where the entry into Jerusalem is also referred to as a sign. The signs point to the gift that is to come, and the gift is the life of Jesus made available for those who believe in him through his exaltation on the cross. The content of the hour is the willing surrender of life, the crucifixion and resurrection, the return of Jesus to the Father, and the gift of the Spirit whereby he lives in his disciples; all this is referred to as the glorifying of the Son of man. And this is said as the answer to the request of the Greeks to see Jesus; there is no other answer, nor is anything further recorded about these Greeks; there did not need to be. They represent the world in so far as the world will believe in Jesus; they will believe through the testimony of those who have become disciples, and through receiving the Spirit.

The hour therefore involves death for Jesus, just as seeds must lose their form as seeds in order to grow and become fruitful. Neither Jesus nor his followers must love their lives in such a way that they try to hang on to them and attempt to preserve them. It is unbelief that protects itself, thinking wrongly that life can be preserved, whereas it is given in order that it may be surrendered for a better, eternal life. This eternal life is what Jesus himself is, and the only way for anyone to have it is to be where Jesus is. John uses the language (which Paul had also used) of sharing the same space, being in. To have eternal life, to be with Christ, to be in him, for him to be with you, and to be honoured by the Father, are all one and the same reality; the purpose of the book is to enable people to participate in it.

John will have no account of Jesus praying in Gethsemane before his arrest, such as the other evangelists record in their gospels. It would have been impossible to pass from the assurance with which Jesus spoke at the supper, and the prayer at the end of the supper, to an account of the agony in the garden. John does, however, include a reference to it at this point instead; he does not want his readers to attend to the human emotions of Jesus, but to the divine life that they receive through him and in him; this life, he believes, is the gift of the Son to his followers, given freely and willingly and without any resentment or restraint. So though Jesus is troubled, he does not ask to be rescued from death; he asks the Father to glorify his name, that is, to reveal himself as the God who loves the world and who wills its salvation and has sent his Son to save it by bringing into existence those who through faith in Jesus have eternal life, and glorify God for his gift.

In the other gospels, there were two occasions in which a voice was heard from heaven: the baptism and the transfiguration. In Mark and Luke, the voice at the baptism was addressed to Jesus, and here in John it is so, too. God answers Jesus, and says that he has glorified his name in the words and deeds of Jesus that John has recorded in the first half of his gospel. The believer can now understand who Jesus is and what he has come to bring, and can praise God for it. But this is only the mid-point of the book and there is more to follow, in which God will again glorify his name, for Jesus will explain the meaning of his death and resurrection, the coming of the Spirit and the union of the Father and the Son with the believer in eternal life through this Spirit; moreover, Jesus' teaching will be followed by action that will bring the new gift to the disciples.

Revelation is always ambiguous; there is no clear vision, or, in this case, audition. The crowd, which now stands for unbelief, hears God's voice merely as thunder, signifying nothing; some say, wrongly, that an angel spoke to Jesus, but this is a double mistake: it was not an angel, and it was not for his sake but for theirs; and as they have not received it, it is for the sake of the reader of the book, the believer who is to be assured that what will take place is all to God's glory.

The hour that has now come is the time when God judges the world and discloses its sin, which is the rejection of Jesus and his crucifixion. But simultaneously this is the moment when Satan loses his power and is excluded from heaven. The lifting up of Jesus from the earth is a portmanteau-expression meaning both his crucifixion and his exaltation to heaven. He takes the place of Satan in the presence of God (Zechariah 3), so that instead of an accuser we have an advocate with the Father, who draws everyone to himself, to give them life and to enable them to be with him where he is. The crowd is presented as unable to understand how a person who has died by crucifixion can also remain for ever to do the things that Jesus says he will do. They lack the key, which is the double sense of lifting up; Jesus has the power not only to lay down his life but also to take it again. They are left, as Nicodemus had been left, asking questions to which no answers are given. The only hope for partial faith such as theirs is to live by the light that it provides. Faith cannot be forced; it needs time to grow and mature, and it must do this at its own pace. The fact that faith is only partial should not be used as an excuse for doing nothing; one must act according to the light one has, or one will cease to have it. And if one asks, then the promise is that faith will grow, and one will be a less imperfect believer.

This section of John's gospel was ostensibly about the Jews preparing themselves for Passover; but it has turned out to be a preparation of the reader of the book for the true Passover which is Christ, his hour and his glorification. John has taken us through the plan to arrest Jesus, the anticipation of his anointing for burial, the raising of the dead, the king's entry into Jerusalem, the conversion of the world and the drawing of everyone to be where Jesus is, that is, in God. The book of signs therefore ends as preparation for that to which the signs point; but before John passes on to the second part of his book, he separates the two parts with a retrospective section, showing that scripture has been fulfilled in what has happened, and providing a final, short summary of the message of Jesus.

12.36b–50 Faith and unbelief

These two paragraphs separate the signs from the glorification of Jesus. In the first, John explains that the unbelief of the Jews fulfils the prophecies of Isaiah in which he had predicted Israel's unbelief and said that God would withhold understanding from his people. And then, in apparent contradiction, John says that many did believe, but did not say so openly because they were afraid of the reprisals that the Pharisees would take; and that this showed the weakness of their faith, because it was motivated by the desire to be praised by men rather than the only true motivation, to be praised by God.

In these seven and a half (36*b*–43) verses John has given us at least three distinct reasons why his contemporaries did not believe: (1) it was predicted in scripture; (2) it was caused by God; and (3) it was the result of fear and love of a false glory. The first and second of these are difficult for the twentieth-century reader; the third, the moral explanation, is easier to understand.

The belief that the events of Jesus and the church were predicted by the prophets hundreds of years before they happened runs through the whole of the New Testament; Christians accepted the scriptures of the Jews as a collection of prophecies of Jesus' conception, birth, miracles, ministry, death, resurrection and ascension, and of the coming of the Holy Spirit. The Qumran community, an ascetic Jewish sect from whom we have the Dead Sea Scrolls, similarly used the prophets as predictions of their movement; and any Jew of the time might have read scripture as foretelling the events at the end of the world. John's use of scripture may be a problem for us, but it would not have caused his contemporaries any difficulty; they would have accepted the legitimacy of his method, whether or not they agreed with the application he made of it in respect of Jesus.

The idea that faith was the activity of God in the believer was also shared by many other New Testament writers; Paul speaks of believers as people who have been chosen by God and called by God; the author of Acts writes of God opening the heart of Lydia to give heed to what Paul was saying, and of the Lord adding to the number of the disciples day by day those whom he was saving. John belonged to a world in which all the important things that happened were done by God, or the devil, or angels, or demons. Faith and its opposite, unbelief, were too important to be left to the decision of the individual: if one believed, it was because God had opened one's eyes; if one did not, it was because God had blinded them.

The important point for the twentieth-century reader may be that John adds the third explanation to the first and the second; he need not have included it; he might have said only that God had foretold it and kept his word. But he does not do that; he adds the statement that many of the authorities believed, and then shows the weakness of this faith that could not cast out fear, but was over-ridden by love of human praise. Divine action takes place in the human will, that either consents and co-operates, or rejects and hardens itself against God. John believes that God knows what we shall decide to do, before we do it; but he does not think that God's foreknowledge limits our freedom. In John's world, explanations that seemed contradictory to later generations could be placed side by side without difficulty.

The other paragraph is a retrospective summary of the essential message of Jesus, as John understands it and as he has been setting it out in his book. Jesus is God's agent, so to believe in him is to believe in the Father; the book is therefore not Christo-centric, but theocentric; Jesus knows himself to be the apostle of God, and declares himself as such. His mission is to bring everyone out of the darkness of the present world which is doomed to death into that light and life that are symbols of union with Jesus and with God through the Spirit. Jesus' primary purpose is to save, not to judge and condemn; those who do not believe make his mission into their condemnation before Christ and before the Father who authorized him. Will there be some who reject Jesus finally and for ever? John did not know any more than we know, but he did believe that the will of the Father is to give eternal life through union with Jesus.

The idea that some people would be eternally damned was found in some Jewish circles and among Christians too; but it should be noticed that it is not mentioned with the same frequency in all the New Testament books; Matthew is the one writer in the New Testament who has a totally disproportionate number of the references to hell; elsewhere they are very infrequent, and the words hades and gehenna never come in John's gospel. John's position is that God wills life for all his creatures, and that this is received through faith in Jesus; God makes faith possible, by giving the believers to the Son, and drawing them towards him. There is unbelief, and there will be condemnation on the last day; but he is surprised that it is so, because the bias is towards life.

13,14 *The beginning of the supper*

We can see how important the death and resurrection of Jesus were to the evangelists, from the way they describe the events of the Friday and Sunday on which they occurred; they do this in far greater detail and at much greater length than in the rest of their gospels. More than a third of John's gospel is devoted to the supper, arrest, trials, crucifixion and resurrection. There is one notable difference, however, between John and his predecessors: they have a final speech of Jesus before the passion and the resurrection narrative begins, but John has his farewell speech of Jesus at the supper itself; moreover, the johannine speech is much longer than those in the other gospels; it is about the same length as the account of the events that follow it.

The speech of Jesus at the supper explains the death and resurrection that follow it, and the gift of the Spirit on Easter day. In the earlier part of the book, the pattern was: signs followed by speeches; here it is the other way round. But John does not provide us with a doctrine of the atonement or a theory that explains the rationale of the death and resurrection; his intention is to move away from a doctrinal understanding of the crucifixion and of the whole situation created by the coming of Jesus towards a way of appropriating it that is more personal and mystical; one might say, he wants us to use our hearts rather than our heads. The truth is Jesus; so the revelation must be a person, not a doctrine. To have the truth one must be in relationship with the person; eternal life is to know God and Jesus Christ, and the final manifestation is their dwelling in the believer. We shall search this part of John in vain for a johannine theory or theological explanation of the cross and resurrection such as we are offered, for example, in The Letter to the Hebrews.

John avoids technical terms such as ransom, sacrifice, atonement, expiation and forgiveness, and he uses instead expressions that state the facts in a clear and straightforward manner: Jesus' death is his going away from the disciples, and his resurrection is his return to them; first they will not see him, then they will see him again; the gift of the Spirit is the arrival of the one who will teach them about Jesus. The johannine language is personal language, it is all in words that describe what people do. This is because the only reality is personal: Jesus himself, and his Father, and the relationship between them and the disciple that the Spirit creates. Jesus brings this relationship into existence by his going and his coming; no further explanation, John believes, is needed; to ask for a further explanation is to miss the point of what Jesus has in fact made available.

It is with theology in this gospel as it is with the sacraments: John believes that both can become a way by which the actual state of affairs is concealed. The truth is the presence of the Father and Jesus Christ, through the Spirit, with the believer. John's insistence on this explains why he has not included the institution of the eucharist in his account of the supper. In its place John has the story of Jesus washing his disciples' feet, and commanding them to wash one another's feet, and to love one another. There is indeed one disciple and only one to whom Jesus gives something to eat during the supper, and this is Judas Iscariot; after he receives the bread, Satan enters into him. If this is intended as a comment on the eucharist, it is strange and severe.

It is appropriate that the institution of the eucharist should be replaced by the footwashing, because there is a theme common to both: in the eucharist, Jesus relates himself to the disciples as food to those who eat it; and in the footwashing as a slave to a master. Both eucharist and foot-washing point to the laying down of life for others, as food, or as slave. We live at the expense of the life of what we eat, and we are made clean by the one who lays aside his garments, symbolizing the laying down of his life. Seen in this way, as the sacramental re-enactment of the death of Jesus at the hands of his followers, the eucharist becomes an embarrassment to them, and we can see why Matthew has added the words, Take this and eat . . . Drink from it, all of you. In the footwashing, similarly, Peter is embarrassed at what Jesus is doing and says, You shall never wash my feet. But just as they must eat and drink in another gospel, so they must accept what Jesus is doing for them here, and allow him to wash their feet, or else they will have no part in him.

The section begins with the statement that Jesus knew that this was the hour that he was due to depart to the Father on the cross, and that he loved his disciples utterly and completely. All that he does and says must be understood as the words and deeds of one who is entirely devoted to the good of others. The rôle of Judas as betrayer is explained by reference to the devil, whose agent Judas becomes; and the mention of the betrayal at this point in the narrative helps us to see the footwashing as the sign of the death of Jesus, the way in which he gives his life to others. Peter's objection to having his feet washed by Jesus in this gospel is similar to his refusal to accept Jesus' prediction that he will fall away in the other gospels, and Jesus' reply in both cases is that he must die for Peter. Peter then mistakes the symbol for the reality and asks to be washed all over, hands and head. Jesus then says, and here it is probably best to follow the shorter text as in RSV margin and NEB text, that what he will do is enough: the sign is the washing of feet, and the reality is his death. This will cleanse Peter and the other disciples; the one exception is Judas Iscariot.

The willingness of Jesus to die for the disciples is to set in motion further acts of the same kind between the disciples themselves; if he who is greater than they has done this for them, how much more should they do it for one another? There is a further reference to Judas Iscariot, who fulfils a passage in the Psalms: the table-companion acts treacherously. But Jesus warns them of what will happen in advance and then they will be able to believe afterwards. The command that disciples should follow the example of their master is balanced by the corresponding promise that those who receive one who has been sent by Christ receive both Christ and the Father. There must therefore be a common likeness running through from Father to Son and to disciples, and this likeness which is love is expressed in the laying down of life for others.

The statement that Jesus was troubled recalls the scene at the tomb of Lazarus and the contrast there between the weeping of Mary and the Jews, and Jesus' demonstration that Lazarus was alive; here too there is a contrast, and it is between the command to lay down one's life, which is the essence of discipleship, and the forthcoming action of one of the disciples, who will hand Jesus over to the authorities. Jesus foretells betrayal by a disciple, and the confusion that this produces among them is the occasion for the introduction of the disciple described as the one Jesus loved. Here, as in most of his appearances in this book (and he is not mentioned in any other), he is nearer to the truth than Peter who appears alongside him. This disciple therefore knows who will be the betrayer, and John makes it clear that he alone of the disciples knows this.

John presents the action of Judas as the result of complex forces: scripture has predicted it, and has been quoted: the moral character of Judas has also been mentioned, that he was a thief; and we have been told that he was a devil, and that Satan had entered into him. John also wants his readers to know that the betrayal by Judas was no surprise to Jesus, but that he had told the beloved disciple in advance; and that Judas acted only when Jesus commanded him to act. In all of this, John wants to safeguard the freedom of Jesus in laying down his life; no one is taking it from him, and he is not unaware of what will happen or unwilling that it should. The references to the devil or Satan are to show that evil is not independent of God and cannot frustrate his will; as in the book of Job, Satan does only what God permits him to do, and Jesus wills his death as the way in which he makes life available to others. Judas goes from the presence of Jesus into the night of darkness and death.

What Judas does brings about the exaltation of Jesus and the revelation of God's glory. Jesus will be seen to be the life-giver, the one who is motivated entirely by love; and God will exalt him to heaven, because he will have completed the work that he came to do.

The ambiguous expression, Where I am going, is explained. There will be a different state of affairs for the disciples, the result of the new way in which Jesus will be with them. His death is a going only in the sense that one way of being present will be exchanged for another. The disciples, like the Jews, cannot follow Jesus to his death; he must do for them what they cannot do for themselves. During the time of his absence (in the very restricted sense of absence that is being used here) they will have one thing only to show to the world, and one commandment only that they must keep: they must love one another, and reproduce among themselves the love with which Jesus has loved them.

Here again we can see the radical nature of John's revision. The disciples of Jesus (he never uses the word church in his gospel, unlike Matthew, and it is best to avoid the word in the exposition of his book, if we possibly can) will be known to the world not by a visible connection or link with Jesus, such as continuity through the laying-on of hands, or continuity of preaching and teaching, or the sacramental tradition, or charismatic phenomena, but only in so far as in union with Jesus they love one another as Jesus loved them, and lay down their lives for one another as Jesus did for them. It is typical of John to reject the external and institutional in favour of the personal. Whether or not we regard what he says as adequate, what he says is that disciples are to be recognized by their love and not by anything else.

The dying of Jesus for them comes first, before they can

follow his example and before his love can be reproduced in them. The conversation with Peter shows the need for the priority of Jesus' death: just as Peter had objected to having his feet washed by Jesus, so now he cannot understand why he may not follow Jesus immediately. He does not yet understand that going means going to the Father through death on the cross. His assertion that he will lay down his life for Jesus is ironical, because he does not realize either that it is in fact a matter of laying down one's life that is being discussed, or that this is precisely what he cannot do yet. The repetition by Jesus of Peter's offer, when he asks Peter, Will you lay down your life for me?, emphasizes the inappropriateness and emptiness of Peter's boast. Far from dying on behalf of Jesus, he will disown him in order to save his skin not only once but three times before dawn.

The only break between Jesus' prediction of Peter's denials and what follows in the next paragraph is the change from singular to plural, from words addressed to Peter alone to words addressed to all the disciples. (The chapter divisions that are now universal were not introduced into Bibles until A.D. 1238 and do not always correspond to breaks in the sense.) Jesus has said that the leader of the disciples will fail, but they are not to be distressed because of this, since their faith is to be in God and in Jesus, not in human beings. The departure of Jesus is for the purpose of preparing a place for the disciples in the life of God, pictured here as a house of many rooms. The death of Jesus makes it possible for the disciples to live with the life of God; and this life is Jesus himself: he will come and take them to himself, and he and they will be united. The language of place stands for union, sharing, fellowship, friendship, and all the other good things that can be enjoyed through being with another person in the same place. In the allegory of the vine, this idea will be expressed through the repetition of the words *abide* and *in*.

Jesus had said that he was going, and Peter had not understood that this meant death; Jesus now repeats that he is going, and says that they know the way. This provokes the question of Thomas which reveals the ignorance of the disciples (and of the readers, of whom the disciples are representations). The answer of Jesus is the sixth of the I AM sayings, and it concentrates our attention on Jesus as the total means of salvation. He is the way, or road, by which the believer walks, that is, he replaces the law of Moses as the way of God's commandments. Jesus is not a teacher of ethics in John's gospel, as he is for example in Matthew's. He teaches only two commandments: to believe in him and to love one another. The way, as John understands it, is not teaching or instructions, but Jesus himself: having him, they have no need of ethics, any more than a ship that has an experienced pilot needs a chart. In the same way, Jesus is the truth; it is not doctrine but a person, and the only way to know the truth is to know him and stay with him. So also with life: the Word is the life, and the disciples will live through their union with him by faith. In the other gospels, life and eternal life belong to the future, the age to come, the kingdom of God and the time after the last judgement; but here it is not necessary to wait for life, because Jesus had returned and taken the disciples to himself, so that they share his life. John has abolished the need for theology and for eschatology, and replaced them with the present, living Christ.

The exclusiveness that is implied in the statement that Jesus is the way to the Father, and that no one comes to the Father except by him is another of the embarrassments that the twentieth-century reader experiences when he reads this book. As in the case of other such offensive passages in John, we may start by noticing that John is not alone among the New Testament writers in expressing this idea; in Acts for example Peter says that there is no other name given under heaven whereby we shall be saved; and Matthew reverses a saying of Jesus in Mark so as to make Jesus say that he who is not for us is against us. Paul assumes that the Galatians only received the Spirit when the gospel was preached to them. What seems to have happened is that awareness of what they had received through faith in Christ and baptism in his name led Christians to make claims for Jesus that were total: all that they had was his gift; in this context, that was all they could say, and they could not be expected to say less. To ask whether those who are faithful to another religion, either before the birth of Christ or after, are in communion with God and partake of his Spirit, is to raise an entirely different question, and to move into a context that calls for other considerations. The language of exclusiveness is not appropriate when we are talking about the love of God for the world and his care for it throughout its history. No one comes to the Father but by me, is the way the Christian believer says what he has found to be true: that union with God is through Jesus. It is the language of faith, love, devotion; not an objective statement of fact intended to prescribe limits for God's love. To understand it in an exclusive sense, as if it meant that all religions other than Christianity were false, is to mistake the way language is being used.

Knowledge of Jesus is knowledge of the Father because the life that Jesus gives is the life that he has received from the Father. The Son is the one who is dependent on the Father, obedient to him, and not one who acts on his own initiative and authority. He is transparent, so that through him we see God who is at work in him.

Philip's request shows up the inadequacy of Philip's faith; he is myopic and must change his focus so as to see through Jesus to the Father. Notice here the use of the word *in*: Jesus is in the Father in the sense that he is dependent on him; the Father is in Jesus, in that he acts through him and has been made visible by the signs that Jesus has done; his life and goodness and power have all been shown in healing, providing food and drink, and giving life. As well as the signs, there have also been the words of Jesus, in which he has spoken of his relationship with the Father; these words have been spoken in obedience to God and through the inspiration of God. It is possible to come to faith in Jesus as God's agent, through his words and deeds, and so receive life from God. Just as Jesus is in the Father and performed signs, so the believer is in Christ and will do signs, and give life to others. In fact the disciple will do greater works than Jesus, because of his death and return to the Father. Here again we are listening to the language of faith, devotion and unlimited expectation. John is saying the same thing as the other evangelists, that all things are possible with God; faith can move mountains and raise the dead; whatever you ask will be given to you. The purpose of the promise of greater works and answered prayer is to express the unrestricted scope of the personal relationship between the Father, the Son and the believer; to apply it to specific situations is to mistake poetry for prose. The emphasis is not on what the believer can demand from God, but on what God will receive from the believer; God will be glorified by the Son and by those who believe in the Son and live in him. The astounding generosity of God will result in extraordinary praise of him.

The result of the death and resurrection of Jesus will be a new situation in which the disciples will be united with Jesus through love and obedience, and God will pour out his Spirit on them, to hold them together and to him, for ever. The Spirit is now given the title Paraclete (RSV Counsellor, NEB Advocate), a term used only in this gospel and 1 John in the New Testament. We shall see what it means from the way it is used. He is the Spirit of truth, because he came upon Jesus at the beginning, and Jesus is the truth; he will reveal the truth to the disciples, in the sense that he will make Jesus known to them. He dwells with them now, because he is the inspiration of Jesus; and he will be in them, because he will inspire the disciples. But he is not to be thought of as a rival or competitor: his function is to make Jesus present and known and effective in the believer. In so far as the disciples are believers already, it is because the Spirit is at work in them; and when he comes on Easter day, as Jesus breathes on them, he will continue to perform the work of mediating Christ to the believer.

The coming of the Paraclete will be the coming of Christ. The believers will see Christ in a non-physical way, and share his resurrection life. Through the Spirit they will understand the situation in which they will then find themselves: Jesus in the

Father, the disciples in Jesus, and Jesus in them; here again the language of locality points to personal relationships of love, obedience, dependence, fellowship and unity. The commandments are to believe and to love, and obedience to them means being the object of the Father's love.

The manifestation of Christ will not be a cosmic event at the end of the world, the coming of the Son of man to judge the living and the dead; but it will be the revelation of Jesus to the believer. Notice here how the plural, which has been used throughout this chapter up to verse 20, is replaced by the singular in verse 21; what is promised is the revelation of Christ to the individual believer, not to the community (as in Matthew), and not to the world. John is replacing the corporate conception of Christian faith such as we find in Paul, who saw the individual believer as a limb or organ of the body, needing others in order to function usefully, with an individualistic faith: each believer is related to Christ one by one, and dependence on other believers is not mentioned.

A Judas who was the son of James was included in the list of the twelve in Luke and Acts; this is presumably the Judas not Iscariot who now asks how this manifestation will take place; his name gives him the title to ask this question, since Judas or Judah is the root of the word Jew in all languages, and it was a commonplace belief among Jews and Jewish Christians (Paul, the other evangelists, and others) that there would be a final judgement of the world, in which God or his agent would reveal himself to everyone, living and dead. This is one of the moments in this book when we can see clearly the difference between John and his predecessors; John is making the nature of his revision apparent in this conversation between Judas and Jesus; a last judgement is no longer to be expected, but the union of the individual believer with the Father and the Son, and this takes place in the present. Waiting is abolished. So is any gospel for the world, any hope of a new earth, the social aspect of Christianity, all that is meant by incarnational Christianity. John's way of thinking is spiritual, internal, mystical and other-worldly.

Many readers of this gospel will look in vain for various aspects of the Christian message in which they firmly believe. They will be glad that if it was John's intention to replace and supersede the other three gospels, or some of them, he did not succeed. We need them, as well as him, for a balanced point of view.

The believer becomes the object of the Father's love, and the Father and the Son will abide in him. The word translated *home* in the RSV is the noun from the verb *abide*, which will be used in the next section of the speech; and it is the same word in Greek which is translated *room* in verse 2 of this chapter. The many rooms in the Father's house are the believers, and the Father and the Son dwell in each room. The local language of *I in you* is being presented pictorially.

The discourse returns to the promise of the Paraclete for the second time; he will teach the disciples all that they need to know, which is all that Jesus has told them. The Paraclete will not add to what has been said, he is not an innovator; Jesus is the truth, and there cannot in any case be additional truths, because the truth is the person; having the truth is being with him.

The foretelling of Peter's denials had caused distress among the disciples; that was how the discourse had begun, and Jesus returns to that theme now. Instead of fear they are to have peace, because they are going to receive the final gift of God, and to be incorporated into the life of the creator of the world. The peace they are to have will be the peace of the final state of blessedness, and they will have it from the moment Jesus returns to them on Easter day; his first words will be, Peace be with you.

Jesus is going to the Father, and all that is good will follow from this. He has told them these things in advance, in order that they may believe; and in order that the reader may understand what he is reading, and have faith. Satan is on the way in the person of Judas Iscariot, but they have nothing to fear from this, because Jesus has commanded him to do what he is about to do, and Jesus too is doing what the Father has commanded him to do. His love, obedience and death will convince the world of who he is and bring it life. Jesus therefore commands his disciples to rise and go with him to the Father's house and to participation in the life of God.

15, 16 *The supper continued*

Jesus has said that he is going; it is necessary to understand the situation that will follow.

The allegory of the vine describes the relationship between the believer, Christ and God, as it will be after the resurrection of Jesus. The disciples will be dependent on Christ, as the branch depends on being in the vine; and the purpose of the relationship is described as bearing fruit. John does not explain what the fruit is, just as he did not specify what the greater works would be; he does not need to do so, because he is writing about eternal life, that new gift that believers have received and that exalts them into a new consciousness and experience of existence. What he means can only be understood from close attention to what he says.

The Greek word that is translated in the RSV by the verb *to prune* means also *to cleanse*, and it is the same word that is translated as *made clean* in verse 3. The disciple has received Christ's revelation of himself, and this is compared to washing, cleansing, the removal of sin and guilt. So one aspect of eternal life is freedom from evil, the forgiveness of sins, release from the inhibiting influence of the past.

A further aspect of eternal life is explained by the word *abide*, which John uses twelve times in the first sixteen verses of this chapter; it is a word that is characteristic of John, and he means by it that the believer is dependent on Christ for the gift of eternal life, and that this can be seen in two ways: the believer is in Christ, and Christ is in the believer. Eternal life is a gift, and it always retains its quality of being received; it is not an inheritance which once accepted may pass into the control of the one who has inherited it; eternal life has to be received from moment to moment without intermission, just as the branch of the vine is always receiving its ability to bear fruit; any break in the connexion would be fatal.

A third way that John uses to describe eternal life is to say that it is like asking and receiving; it provides access to one who is totally available and attentive and at your disposal. Just as Herod promised Salome anything she asked, to half his kingdom, because she pleased him, so the believer pleases God, and he will give him whatever he asks for. The intention of saying that all requests will be answered is to express the sense of being the object of another's delight; it would therefore be a mistake to put the idea into reverse and start from the question, Why are prayers not answered?

Another aspect of eternal life is obedience to commands, particularly the commands to believe in Jesus and love one another. Eternal life is not a gift that can be detached from the one who gives it; nor does it isolate the one who has received it from others. Giver and gift are identical, and the way in which Christ is present in the gift of himself to the believer is always as the one who is to be obeyed. At this point we see how John has modified the tendency towards individualism in his writing, by insisting on mutual love.

It is essential also to understand that eternal life is joy. Paul had said so too; the fruit of the Spirit was love and joy. Luke describes the joy of the believers in Acts. Here in John it is first the joy of Jesus because he has brought it into the world and made it possible for others to receive it; also because it is not the believer's selfish or private joy, but the joy of another into which he has been drawn; and it is only secondly the joy of the believer, because it is not centred on himself, but is what is external to him, really desired and totally satisfying.

To find yet another way of trying to describe eternal life, John turns to friendship. The believers are not servants of Christ, but friends. His death has constituted them as his friends, as has also the teaching that he has given them: they know what he intends, and he has revealed his secrets to them, as one would not do to slaves. But John will not let us think that friendship with Jesus puts the believer on a level of equality with him; he has chosen them, appointed them and he commands them. John's understanding is very different from ours: to us, friendship and the giving of orders are two quite separate contexts; it was not so for him.

The position of the believer therefore is one of privilege and honour; eternal life is the greatest gift that could ever be received by a human being; it is participation in God's life, and union with him and with Christ. Everything that could ever be desired is fulfilled and surpassed in eternal life: it is joy, access to God, cleansing, friendship with Christ and knowledge of his will. John wants his readers to know this and to share it; he has written his book for this purpose, perhaps because he felt that previous gospels had not made the point clearly enough.

But we must notice that John is always guarding against possible misunderstandings; he is saying it would be a mistake to think that eternal life gave one independence of God, or of Christ, or of other believers. There is always dependence and receiving. The believer is under orders to abide and to love; his status is not the result of his own choosing, but of being chosen, and this quality of eternal life, expressed through the use of the passive verbs, must never be lost to sight.

John then turns to the situation in which the believers will find themselves in the world, and he describes it in terms of hatred. The world is opposed to Jesus, and it will be opposed to his followers too; they will be persecuted. By the world, John means all that does not accept God or understand itself as creature, made by a creator. The essential quality of the world is the attempt to live out of oneself and for oneself, and the organizations and arrangements that follow from it. The world is totally opposed to Jesus, because he is the one who has demonstrated dependence on God finally and definitively. His coming into the world has caused the world to sin, because he has provided the classic occasion on which the world was able to reject dependence on God by not believing in its own creator, or in the Father who had sent him.

In the third reference to the Paraclete, Jesus tells the disciples that they are to bear witness to the world in their conflict with it, just as he has done. The Paraclete will continue to do in them what he has done through him. They will testify that God is the creator and lord of everything; in return they will be hated and persecuted.

The departure of Jesus should be seen as the occasion for rejoicing; and it will be understood in that way, if its purpose is remembered. Sorrow is unbelief; joy is the proper fruit of faith. The death of Jesus makes it possible for him to return to the disciples in the new way which is the coming of the Paraclete; this is why his death is necessary, and why it will benefit the disciples. But inevitably it will create a tension between them and the world: faith and unbelief struggle with one another. Just as unbelief will persecute faith and try to destroy it, so faith will show up unbelief and try to demolish it.

There are three ways in which this conflict can be seen. First, faith will accuse unbelief of the sin it has committed in putting Jesus to death; this is the capital sin and the essence of all evil, because it is the rejection of the truth that the world is created and that there is a God. Secondly, faith will show that Jesus was right, and that God endorsed his mission and vindicated him in the resurrection; he is now invisible because he is with the Father, and those who believe in him without seeing him believe in his authenticity and are thereby themselves authenticated by the Father. Thirdly, faith condemns the world for what it has done and proclaims that it should be renounced.

As we read these chapters of this book we become extremely aware of the difference between it and the other gospels. There is far more of the author's understanding of Jesus here than there was in them. John knows this, too; how could he not? But he does not explain it as we would; he does not speak of himself as an individual with a peculiar background in Jewish and Hellenistic religious thought and insight. John's explanation why his book contains new and different material from the other gospels is by means of his understanding of the Spirit. The work of the

Spirit is to explain Jesus who is the truth, and he has no other purpose. The things to come that he will declare to the disciples are the crucifixion, the resurrection and the gift of the Spirit. According to John there is no other work of the Spirit than this, and this way of thinking about the Spirit is typically johannine. If the truth is a person, then knowledge of that person is all that is meant by knowing the truth; that is what it is to receive the revelation and to hear and keep the word. The Spirit attaches the believer to Jesus by making him known to him; and because Jesus is the Word of God, the believer is related to the Father also. Eternal life is to know God and Jesus Christ whom he has sent. John believes that the Spirit has spoken to him, giving him this insight into his working. What John says about the Spirit explains how John understood what he was doing in writing this new and very different gospel. If we had asked John, Why is your book so unlike the other three? he would have answered, Because the Spirit guided me to write in this way.

Belief in the Spirit as the cause of inspiration and the power that made disciples into witnesses was not without foundation in the earlier tradition; Mark had recorded a saying of Jesus that promised that the Holy Spirit would speak, and that disciples were not to be anxious what to say when they were put on trial for their faith. John is in effect claiming the fulfilment of this promise in the writing of his book. We know from what is perhaps the oldest Christian writing that has survived (1 Thessalonians) that Christians believed that they spoke under the influence of the Spirit, but also that what was said had to be tested. The claim to be inspired and the need to discriminate were not thought of as mutually exclusive: faith was to be neither credulous nor sceptical. John's test for knowing what is the work of the Spirit is whether what is said makes Jesus known and effects union with him.

One of the devices John uses to draw attention to a point is the frequent repetition of a single word or phrase; we had an example of it at the beginning of this section of the gospel, where emphasis was made by reiteration of the verb *abide*. Now we have the same method, with the single Greek word that is translated *a little while*; it comes seven times in five verses, and the repetition forces the reader to attend to what is being said. There are two *little whiles* separated by the going to the Father; the meaning of this is that the length of time till Jesus will see them again after his going is of the same order as the short time before he goes; or to put it prosaically, in less than twenty-four hours he will be dead; in a further forty-eight hours they will see him again. Easter will be the day when they will rejoice, and from then on no one will be able to deprive them of their joy, his life shared with them. Seeing will be believing, and there will be no need for asking, because their joy will be complete. But John delights in paradox: asking will be receiving, because there will be no limitations or qualifications to the union and unity of the Father, the Son and the believer.

The section ends ironically: Jesus says that he has used figures of speech, but that soon he will tell them about the Father without figures but by actions: his death and resurrection and the giving of the Spirit. This will effect the union that he has spoken about: speech will give place to deeds. But the disciples misunderstand him; they see Jesus as merely one who knows what is going to happen, a messenger from God and no more. They think they have understood, and that Jesus has made everything clear to them. But we know that like the woman in childbirth they must go through sorrow, weeping and lamentation; they cannot know the truth until the events have happened, and this will include Peter's denials and the scattering of all the disciples. To the question, Do you now believe? they should have answered, No. The events which are about to take place will be greater than the prediction of them, and will shatter the disciples. But it will not shatter him, because his union with the Father will remain firm throughout, and that is the ground of their peace: Jesus and the Father constitute the base on which the disciple stands; the obedience of Jesus to the Father is the victory that will be shared with the believers.

We see here very clearly the sharp difference between John and

Mark. In Mark, though Jesus had predicted his death, he is overcome with sorrow when the hour arrives; and his final words are My God, my God, why have you forsaken me? Jesus dies in darkness, mocked by everybody. In John on the other hand there will be no mocking during the crucifixion, no darkness and no cry of dereliction. In Mark, Jesus himself experiences the difference between the event as it was predicted and the event as it is perceived; in John, it is the disciples who experience the difference. In Mark, the irony works against Jesus; in John, against the disciples.

But though the picture in Mark is very different from John's, the intention of both writers is the same: they both mean to say that we live because of Jesus. In Mark, this is said by showing how he gave his life as a ransom for many, the food by which they live; in John, by showing that he has done what the Father commanded, and has made life available for everybody.

17 *The supper concluded*

The end of the discourse at the supper is a prayer; Jesus turns from addressing his disciples to addressing the Father. This is what John means when he says, He lifted his eyes to heaven. The importance of this for understanding this section of the gospel, and the gospel as a whole, cannot be exaggerated. John has prepared for it by showing that the disciples do not yet believe; in fact their situation is even worse than that, because they think they do believe. This false confidence must be broken before they can receive what is being offered to them; so Jesus must pray for them. The same idea is found in Luke's gospel, where Jesus says during the supper that he has prayed for Peter.

He is praying for them that they may have the joy which is eternal life while they are still in the world, sent into it by Jesus in order that others may believe through their preaching. The answer of the Father to the prayer of Jesus will be the gift of eternal life. Those who receive it know that it is a gift, given to them at the request of the Son to the Father. This is not meant to imply that the Father is unwilling to give the gift, or that he has to be persuaded by the Son; John explicitly denies any such idea: the Father loves them; they are the Father's gift to the Son. There is, however, a good reason for seeing eternal life as the answer of the Father to the Son's prayer: it shows that what is received is entirely undeserved, and that it cannot be presumed upon, or made into a possession. It is always to be received; we shall think of it best if we always think that it is what we are now about to receive, in answer to the prayer of Jesus.

In the other gospels, Jesus prayed that the hour might pass him by, but here he says that it has come, and asks that what it contains may happen. The Son is to be glorified and to glorify the Father; he will be glorified by being lifted up on the cross and simultaneously exalted to the Father, and he will glorify the Father by making the divine life available to the believers, the elect, those whom the Father has given to the Son. The life is the Son, and the only way to have it is to know him; since he is the agent of God, it is necessary to know both sender and the one who has been sent. Jesus has done all that could and needed to be done to reveal who he is to the elect; now he will return to the Father, and he prays for this to happen. John wants us to see the crucifixion as accepted and willed by Jesus; the other evangelists meant this too, but they approached it in a different way, making the acceptance of the hour a deliberate decision of Jesus in Gethsemane.

A key word in John's account of the prayer is *name*; it comes four times, and it means character, power and authority. Jesus has revealed God to those whom God had chosen and given to him; this revelation is called a word, that is a communication between two rational beings; the content of this word is that Jesus is entirely dependent upon the Father and has no existence in himself or apart from the Father's will. To know Jesus is to know one who is from God, and thus to know God.

The believers are in the world and therefore subject to temptation and persecution; the Son prays that they may be preserved, through the power of God, in his possession. The Father and the

Son are one: the Father being the origin and giver, the Son being the receiver. The believers are to be brought into this unity that exists between the Father and the Son, through the word of Jesus and the power of God. During his time in the flesh, Jesus has been present with them, and able to keep them in God's possession and safe from evil; he prays that this will continue, even when he is not present in the same way. The only one of the disciples who was lost was Judas, and he was a special case because his destiny had been foretold in scripture. Jesus' power to keep his disciples from falling away, and the prayer which he is praying in their presence, will assure them of the mightiness that is working for them, and give them confidence that they have eternal life and joy, even when they are being hated and persecuted by the world.

Why are they not to go with Jesus to the Father immediately? Partly because they are not yet able to follow; but also because they have a work to do in the world; Jesus is sending them into it, in order that they may bear witness to him, and thus bring others to faith. John's understanding is that there are children of God scattered throughout the world, people who are chosen, the elect, the gift of the Father to the Son; but they do not know it yet. They will only know through believing, and believing depends on the word of the disciples (just as the faith of the disciples depended on the testimony of the Baptist, through whom, as John has already said, all believe). Jesus prays for those whom the disciples will convert, that they may have this life that is unity with God, such as Jesus himself shares with the Father. John's hope is that the unity of the believers with Christ and God will convince the world and persuade them to believe in Jesus; only faith can create faith, and only love can produce love.

Jesus keeps nothing to himself; even his glory, which is to bring life to the dying, even this he gives to believers, so that the world may know what love is. They will in the end come to be with God and Jesus in the Father's house, and they will see the glory that he has always had with the Father, namely his giving life to the world.

This is the purpose and end of everything as John understands it. He is one of the very few writers in the New Testament who look forward to going to heaven and express hope in this way. The writer to the Hebrews and the author of The Letter to the Ephesians are probably the only others who share this kind of hope; the majority believe in the coming of God's reign upon the earth, to make a new world here that the meek will inherit. Going to heaven became more and more common as the usual way of thinking, because Christianity was moving away from its Jewish origins; even though the prayer for the coming of the kingdom and the doing of God's will on earth was still being said. John had no conception of a restored earth; his interest was only in persons, human and divine, and not in their environment.

The prayer ends with a statement of the situation before the crucifixion: the unbelief of the world, the knowledge and faith of Jesus, the needs of the disciples to whom Jesus has revealed God's authority and character. He will reveal it again and finally in laying down his life; that will show his intention to share his life with them; that is, his love for them, which is also the Father's love for them; and this love will enfold Father, Son and believer in unity. This is what is prayed for by Jesus, and to be received as the answer to prayer by believers. To them it will always have the quality of a gift to be received, and never an accomplished fact. It will not be demonstrated by a visibly united congregation or by miracle-working individuals, but by those who through faith create faith in others, and by loving draw others into love.

18.1–14 *The arrest*

John tells the same story as the other evangelists of the arrest, crucifixion and resurrection, but he tells it in his own way. It is unlikely that he recounts anything simply because it happened, or for no other reason than that it was in the tradition that he had received; everything in this book is included because it is significant, though we may not always know whether we have caught his meaning. There is an example of this in the account of the arrest: Why does he tell us that the high priest's servant was called Malchus? One suggestion is that he had worked it out from a prophecy of Zechariah, which he may have understood thus: I will deliver them into the hand of Malko. But we have no means of knowing.

John wants to set the tone for the whole story of the crucifixion at the very beginning, and he does so by re-writing the earlier accounts of the arrest. He omits the struggle of Jesus to accept God's will, the prayer that the cup be taken from him, and the contrast between the sleeping disciples and the praying Christ. Instead of asking that the cup be removed, he says to Peter, Shall I not drink it? and the double negative in Greek shows that an affirmative answer is required. As John tells the story, Jesus is in total control of the situation, and he needs no help or support: he does not pray, and he does not ask his disciples to stay awake with him. He knows what is about to happen, and he identifies himself to those who have come to arrest him: he secures the release of his companions, exactly as he had predicted in the prayer to the Father. John wants his readers to understand the story in a particular way; that is why he tells it as he does. Jesus' death was voluntary, and for others, in order that they might have life.

There is obvious irony is the contrast between the band of Roman soldiers and Jewish temple police with their lanterns, torches and weapons, and Jesus who is willing to drink the cup. They have to be helped to do what they have come to do by Jesus himself; he asks them whom they are looking for; he identifies himself twice; he has to overcome their apparent inability to do anything against him of themselves; added to this there is the further irony that they then bind him.

It is not at all clear why John says that Jesus was taken to Annas the father-in-law of the high priest, whom he seems to refer to as though he were the high priest; it is also strange that there is no account of the trial before Caiaphas. Some of the manuscripts of John's gospel have a different order of sentences here, but that may be only an attempt to clear up the problem, to which there is no entirely satisfactory solution.

18.15–27 The high priest's house

John arranges his account of Jesus before the high priest in a way that is reminiscent of Mark's gospel at the same point; he begins with Peter's first denial, then turns to Jesus before the high priest; we know from what Jesus has said to Peter that he will disown him twice more, but we are made to wait for this part of the story while the high priest questions Jesus about his disciples. He replies that he should ask those who heard him about his teaching; we know that Peter is unable to admit that he is a disciple.

There is a complication in John's story that is not found in the other gospels: another disciple as well as Peter, not named, not referred to as the disciple whom Jesus loved, is present in the high priest's house. It is probably the beloved disciple that is meant; he is usually with Peter, as here. This disciple is known to the high priest and arranges for the entry of Peter into the courtyard. The girl who is portress then asks if Peter too is not a disciple, meaning perhaps that she knows that the other man is one of them; and Peter, unlike his companion, says that he is not. John is using the story that Mark and his successors had used, and adapting it. Mark's gospel was thought to be the reminiscences of Peter; John is writing a book that claims to have the authority of a disciple who was superior to Peter: he did not disown Jesus in the high priest's courtyard, he stayed near the cross during the crucifixion, he heard the words of Jesus and took the mother of Jesus to his own home. Maybe we should see John as providing material to answer the question, Why is your book so different from Mark's (i.e., Peter's)? It is better, he is saying, because it is by a disciple who was more faithful than Peter; he is the one whom Jesus loved.

John is more interested in describing the trial before Pilate, the

Roman governor, than the trial before the high priest; and this may be because he believes that the decision of the Jewish court has already been taken in the absence of Jesus; all that was needed was to arrest Jesus and hand him over to the Romans. Nevertheless, he represents the high priest as asking questions about Jesus' disciples and his teaching, and Jesus answers that his work has always been done in public, therefore anyone can bear witness. This answer is regarded as lacking in reverence for the office of the high priest, and one of the officers strikes him – a detail that fulfils a prophecy of Isaiah in the Greek version, I gave my cheeks to blows. The retort of Jesus shows up the confusion of those who do not believe; they lack the clarity of faith and of the truth (the man who had been born blind, for example). There is no answer to Jesus' question, how could there be? Peter's second and third denials and the crowing of the cock bring to fulfilment the prediction that Jesus had made, and confirm his statement that Peter could not follow him. The three questions that Jesus will ask Peter in the Appendix to the gospel, chapter 21, may be intended to correspond to the three denials and to re-instate Peter as pastor of the flock.

18.28–19.16 *The praetorium*

John's account of Jesus before Pilate is an example of his dramatic writing at its most skilful. Three parties are involved: Pilate, the Jews and Jesus. The Jews remain outside the building, and Jesus is sometimes inside with Pilate, sometimes outside and thus in full view of the Jews. The Jews refuse to enter because they want to retain their ceremonial purity in order to celebrate the Passover; the irony is that Jesus is the Passover, and they are seeking his death.

A notable feature of the johannine story is the unwillingness of the Jews to state any charge against Jesus (a detail he may have taken from Mark); it is this that makes Pilate ask what the accusation against him is; but their reply is still evasive: they would not have brought him to Pilate had he not been a criminal. Pilate has to force them to be explicit, and in the end they say that he made himself the Son of God. We know that this is a misrepresentation of what Jesus has said: he is indeed the Son of God, but not of his own making. The only kind of status that unbelief can envisage is that which depends on power; Jesus did not collaborate with those who wanted to make him king by force; he is what he is from God and only from God; but unbelief cannot admit such an idea. Pilate has to goad the Jews into making their accusation, and similarly the Jews have to work on Pilate to make him perform their will. The working out of the tension between these two parties gives the passage its dramatic power.

Pilate's unwillingness to move against Jesus is indicated first by his suggestion that the Jews should try him themselves: they have their law and they can use that. The answer of the Jews raises an apparently insoluble historical problem about the right of the Jews to practise capital punishment under the Roman occupation. What John is primarily interested in, however, is that Jesus had foretold his death by being lifted up, and that this referred to crucifixion, the Roman form of execution, not to stoning, which was the Jewish method. There is also an ironical sense to the Jews' answer, in that it was indeed unlawful for them to put Jesus to death, and yet this was precisely what they were hoping to persuade Pilate to do.

There is another possible link with Mark's account of the trial before Pilate, in the sudden and unexplained question of Pilate, Are you the king of the Jews? Here, however, the point is taken further, and Jesus asks him how he came to ask such a question; the suggestion seems to be that like the high priest earlier in the gospel Pilate is not speaking of his own accord, but as a witness to the truth without realizing it. The questioning then turns to what it is that Jesus has done that has made his people and their leaders hand him over to the Roman governor.

The answer of Jesus is sometimes translated as My kingdom is not of this world (*e.g.* AV, RV), and this text is then used to prove that Jesus was not involved in politics, so neither should the church be. The original Greek does not mean this at all; it is a statement about how Jesus has come to be king; the origin of his status is not the world; he is not from below; he does not derive his authority from the world, but he is from God; God has given him authority to give life, and that is what makes him king. The words translated *of this world* are literally *from this world*.

If Jesus were a ruler whose authority came from below, through the support of the crowd or of the army, then he and his followers would use force to defend him; but as we saw at the arrest, this is not the case. John did not expect there to be a time when the followers of Jesus would engage in war and claim that they were doing it in the name of Christ; nor did he foresee that the movement that was inspired by Jesus would become an institution that used force to achieve its ends. John would in fact have agreed with those who misquote this passage, but for a different reason: his religion was other-worldly, spiritual and individualist, and had no room for application to the re-ordering of life in the present.

Although Jesus is not a king in any sense that makes him a threat to the political authorities, he is a king in the sense which he defines: he bears witness to the truth; and his subjects are those whom the Father has given to him, who hear his voice and have his word. His one function is to reveal the truth: that everything is from God; that he is the one sent by God; that he gives life to the dying by associating them with himself; that he is the truth. Pilate's question therefore, What is truth? is ironical from the reader's point of view: he asked what the truth was, as he was going from its presence to those who were not of the truth.

John uses the Barabbas incident, known to us from the other gospels (though apparently the custom is never mentioned elsewhere in the literature about the Roman Empire), to show yet again the unwillingness of Pilate to do what the Jews want him to do; and this in turn provokes the Jews to reveal their intentions more clearly; they prefer Barabbas to Jesus, and Barabbas was a freedom fighter (the word translated 'robber' is a technical term for a nationalist leader); they side with those who use force to achieve, as they think, the will of God.

Jesus is scourged and dressed in purple like an emperor (the word translated *king* was used of emperors by those who spoke Greek) and crowned with thorns (in mock imitation of the crowns on the heads of emperors on coins of the period) and announced by Pilate, who says that he can find no crime in him; Rome can put up with such a poor attempt at a revolt as this; Pilate is again deliberately mocking the Jews and their supposed king. As in Mark and the other gospels, the incident is highly charged, because the reader believes that Jesus is king, though not in the way that Pilate means; but whereas in Mark the irony is against Jesus, in John it is also against the Jews; they are mocked for bringing Jesus before Pilate and for having no king of their own.

This forces the Jews into a further attempt to persuade Pilate to act as they want, and they do it by introducing the charge that he claimed to be Son of God; this has its effect on Pilate, and he becomes very frightened. He goes in with Jesus and asks what John regards as the proper question, Where are you from? We know that the answer is that Jesus is from God; but this cannot be said to Pilate because he does not deal in these ideas; so Jesus is silent. Pilate speaks of his power, but Jesus replies that Pilate's power is from above, from God and from the emperor; Pilate is an office-holder, and his power goes with his office; Jesus would not have come within Pilate's area of authority, had he not been handed over to him by Judas and the Jews.

Pilate then makes his final bid to set Jesus free, and this provokes the Jews into playing their last card, which is a trump. Pilate's relationship with the emperor will be what eventually determines the case. Pilate has used the title king of Jesus, therefore he is committed to executing him; if he does not do so, the Jews can delate Pilate to Caesar for inefficiency and disloyalty. The Jews have him in their power, because Pilate and the emperor are both part of a system that works in this way; Pilate is simply the delegate of Tiberius, and must act in the way that the law prescribes; he has no freedom.

But Pilate will not go down without one further move; he had announced Jesus to the Jews as *the man*; now, in a more solemn manner, sitting on the judgement-seat, he announces him as *your king*. The Jews repeat their demand for crucifixion, and Pilate mocks them again: it is not proper for them to ask him to crucify their emperor. They then make their final statement of their position, that they are loyal members of the Roman empire, who claim no special status that differentiates them from other nations; they are not in fact God's people, and God is not their king; they have no emperor but Tiberius Caesar.

The reason for the reluctance both of the Jews and of Pilate to act openly is now revealed. They had hoped that it could remain hidden, and that the matter could be dealt with without revealing the truth. But the truth will out in the end. The truth about Pilate is that he is caught in a web of motives and aims that reveal him finally as one who can only respond to the need to protect himself, and in this respect he is in the same position as the high priest (chapter 11); and the truth about the Jews is that in order to achieve the destruction of the one who is the real king, they must abandon the covenant that God had made with them and declare themselves free of all obligations except those which they have to the Roman emperor. Pilate is reduced to the status of a minion, and the Jews to that of any other subjugated people in the empire.

19.17–42 Golgotha

John's account of the crucifixion is shorter than those of the other evangelists, and some of the details that they included are not repeated here: there is no mocking of Jesus, for example, no darkness, no centurion, no bitter cry of dereliction. John has already given us the saying of Jesus that is to interpret his death and control the way in which it is described: no one takes his life from him, but he lays it down of his own accord. He is not acted upon by others, as is so noticeable in Mark, but he is the subject of the action, in control of events, knowing in advance everything that is to happen, and willing it to be accomplished.

The actual time between crucifixion and death is shorter in John than in Mark, and even in Mark it was so brief that Pilate was amazed; in Mark, the crucifixion was at 9 a.m. and the death of Jesus at 3 p.m., but in John he is still before Pilate at mid-day, and dies in time to be buried before evening.

If we read John's account of the crucifixion as it stands, without trying to harmonize it with the other gospels, and take his book as though it were the only gospel there was, we shall be more likely to hear what John meant, and we shall certainly hear a different message from what the other evangelists have to tell. Or it may be we should read John as the deliberate correction of Mark. In any case it will not be that Christ suffered for us; he was made sin on our behalf; the reproaches of those who reproached thee fell on me; it will not be the righteous sufferer of the Psalms, though the Psalms will be quoted; but the Lord who is the creator of all things has come to give them life; he has come to do a work in obedience to the Father, and he does it by making over his life to others by laying it down. This is the act of love which he does for his friends, and he does it majestically and in full awareness of what he is doing.

It is in accordance with this that John tells us that Jesus carried the cross himself, without any assistance from Simon of Cyrene, who is not mentioned; the two others to be executed with Jesus do not mock him, as in Mark, but demonstrate the freedom with which Jesus lays his life down: their lives have to be terminated, his does not, because he has already died. Pilate, who had been tricked by the Jews into ordering the crucifixion to take place, now has his final revenge on them by using the notice that was customarily placed on or near a cross to explain the reason for the execution, as a further way of mocking them. This is the only kind of king that the Romans will allow the Jews to have; this is what happens to anyone who wants to set himself up as the leader of a revolution. The Jews naturally object, and propose an alteration to the text, to make it that being king was only a claim that Jesus made; they imply that he was a false claimant. But Pilate will not change what he has written, because he wants to humiliate the Jews; he is again the unwitting agent of God and he bears witness to the truth.

John retains the fulfilment of the Psalm concerning the division of the clothes, and adds a detail the other evangelist did not have: there was a seamless tunic that was not divided, but the soldiers decided whose it should be by dicing for it. So the two lines of the verse from the Psalm were fulfilled exactly, partition and casting lots. The soldiers, like Pilate, act freely, but what they do is in accordance with God's will, made known through David centuries before. The same incident reads differently in the other gospels: there, it is part of the insult that is being done to Jesus; but here it is an aspect of his glorification; it was to fulfil the scripture, that was why the soldiers did it.

In Mark, the curtain in the temple was torn in two from top to bottom; in John the tunic that was woven in one piece from top to bottom was not torn. Mark is showing us the end of Judaism; John the new order that is perfect, the unity of God and humanity.

In Mark it was said that the women who had followed Jesus from Galilee stood at a distance from the cross looking at what was taking place, and Mark's allusion may have been to the Psalm, My kinsfolk keep far away; but here in John it is different, because his mother and her sister and the other women are standing near the cross, and so is the disciple whom Jesus loved. The way we read this passage will depend on how we understand John's book as a whole; if we take it as largely historical reminiscence, this will be information about the arrangements that Jesus made for his mother shortly before he died; if we take John as a book of good news this is much more than the thoughtfulness of a dying man, and what we have is a statement of the new relationship between Judaism and the followers of Jesus; the future of the synagogue lies with the disciples. We saw how Nicodemus was told that he must be born again, and that there was no continuity between Judaism and the kingdom of God. The same idea may be contained in this incident, if we read the mother of Jesus as representative of the believing Jews, and the disciple whom Jesus loved as the archetypal follower of Jesus. The disciple takes her to his home, and the Jews must leave their institutions and join those who have been banned by their officials.

The account of the supper had begun with the statement that Jesus knew that the hour had come and that God had given everything into this hands; he knew what he had come to do in obedience to the Father, to give life to those at the point of death and salvation to the lost. Now, as we come to the end of the account of the hour, there is another reference to the knowledge of Jesus. He knows that everything has been done that needed to be done; he has revealed God to the world and shown how everyone can be brought into union with God. To fulfil another Psalm (They gave me vinegar when I was thirsty) he says, I thirst, and is given the sour wine; and just as in the Psalm vinegar is meant to be understood as an inappropriate drink to give to one who is thirsty, so here the thirst of Jesus is not for drink of any kind, but for God and the completion of the work of drawing everyone to him. Those who fill the sponge with the sour wine misunderstand what is really meant, but the reader knows because he has heard the prayer of Jesus to the Father for the disciples and for those who will believe because of them; when all have been brought into the unity of the Father and the Son, then the thirst of Jesus will be satisfied.

He has said that he must lay down his life; this is the command he received from his Father, and this is also what his love for his friends leads him to do. If he dies, he will bear fruit in the lives of others, because he will be in them, and they will live through him. He had said that he must go, in order that the Spirit might come, and the evangelist had commented that the Spirit was not yet, because Jesus was not yet glorified. All that needs to be done, therefore, is for him to surrender his life; his final word is, It is completed; he says this, bows his head and hands over the Spirit.

John and the other evangelists do not agree on the date of the crucifixion; all agree that it was on a Friday, but they do not agree on whether the Passover was on the Thursday evening, before the crucifixion (so Mark, *etc*) or on the Friday evening after it (so John). The need to remove the bodies from the crosses is the more urgent in John, because of the beginning of the festival; and the Jews who are keeping it therefore ask Pilate for permission to break the legs of the three victims, and thus hasten their death; but this reveals what is special about Jesus, that he has died already, voluntarily. The piercing of his side, recorded in this gospel only, discloses another aspect of his death: not only is it voluntary, it is also according to the prophecies, that is, according to the will of God: he has died without a bone being broken; he has been pierced, and those who pierced him will see him as judge and saviour and lord, because from the side of Jesus come blood and water. John draws his reader's attention to this; he says there was one who saw it and testified, and he presumably means the disciple whom Jesus loved. Since he makes so much of the event, it must be that he regarded it as specially significant, revelatory, emblematic of the meaning of the event. Water has been used to symbolize eternal life earlier in the book, and the blood of Jesus has also been mentioned as the drink that confers life. What the soldier does with the spear to demonstrate that Jesus is dead shows instead that he is the giver of life. The stab with the spear stands for death, but blood and water stand for life. The seed that dies bears much fruit.

From time to time in his gospel, John has referred to characters who had an imperfect and inadequate faith; they clarified the true meaning of what was to be believed, by not believing and expressing incomplete faith. Joseph and Nicodemus do this now. Joseph can only be a secret disciple, because he fears the Jews; Nicodemus had come to Jesus by night and he is still in the dark, as we can see from the quantity of spices that he brings. They follow the burial customs of the Jews, but the reader knows that in this case the procedure is unnecessary, partly because Jesus has already been anointed for burial at Bethany, but also because he will rise on the third day. Nevertheless, whatever is done to Jesus only serves to reveal his glory all the more; the linen cloths will be evidences of his resurrection and the new and empty tomb will point to his having taken his life again, as he had foretold.

Notice how the word *Jews* is repeated in this final paragraph: fear of the Jews, burial customs of the Jews, the day of preparation of the Jews. The burial is carried out by those who act more from unbelief than from faith; but in the good providence of God this points to the truth and makes it possible to see what is to be believed: that the Son of man has been glorified; life has not been destroyed; it is waiting to be given to others.

20.1–23 The first day

The reader of John's gospel now has to see his story through the eyes of those who at this point in the narrative are not yet believers. It is the need to change one's focus that can create a sense of awkwardness at the end of the book. John had reached such a high level with the statement, I have overcome the world, and with, It is finished, that it is difficult not to find what follows here an anti-climax. John continues his narrative, as the other evangelists had done, though he does so for a different reason: the resurrection stories were necessary for them, because they showed how God reversed the humiliation of Jesus on the cross; in John no such reversal is needed, because there has been no humiliation; all that is needed is to tell the readers how the followers of Jesus became believers, and it is to do this that John continues with resurrection stories.

The tension in these accounts is between what the readers know and what the characters do not know. We notice, for example, how Mary Magdalene assumes that the removal of the stone from the tomb, which is all she can see in the dark, means that someone has removed the body; and this is so, but not in the sense that she means. We notice also that she refers to Jesus as the Lord without knowing that he is Lord now in a new way: he is about to ascend to the Father. The two characters who take over the narrative from her gradually reveal more and more of the situation; the disciple who comes first sees the linen cloths, while Peter who comes second enters the tomb and sees the napkin by itself. The other disciple enters second, but believes first; and John makes the point that they had not previously believed in the necessity for the resurrection either through their understanding of scripture or through the words of Jesus.

Of all the resurrection stories in the New Testament, this is the only one in which the faith of one of the disciples begins on the evidence of the empty tomb, without an appearance of the risen Christ. The disciple whom Jesus loved is unique in believing because he sees the sign, not Jesus; and it is not said here that Peter believed. The earliest Easter stories were of appearances, and these are listed by Paul, who had received the tradition from others. It is only later, in Mark, for the first time as far as we know, that empty tomb stories began to be told, but they were not told as accounts of how faith began – certainly not in Mark's gospel, where the result of finding the tomb empty is fear, amazement and disobedience to the message. Matthew seems to have recognized this, and included an appearance to the women to reinforce the command of the angel. In Luke, too, the important part of the story is the appearances, at Emmaus, to Peter, and in Jerusalem; this outweighs the description of the women finding the tomb empty.

So also here in John: the beloved disciple's faith without seeing Jesus is unique. It is not communicated to Mary Magdalene; she stays outside the tomb, weeping, and when she looks into it she only repeats what she had said to the two disciples, as though nothing had happened in between. This sets the scene for the first of John's appearance-stories, in which he uses the device of misunderstanding to effect: she asks Jesus if he has carried himself away! His statement that he is ascending to the Father takes us one step further in our understanding of what is to be believed; all that he had said about going to the Father will be fulfilled, and all that he had promised to his disciples of eternal life, union with him, the indwelling of the Father and the Son in the believer will also be fulfilled, because his Father will be their Father, his God their God. When Mary Magdalene says, I have seen the Lord, she uses the same title for Jesus that she had used before she believed, but now she uses it in its proper sense.

For his third incident on this first day of the week, John again introduces characters who are not yet believers; the disciples are behind shut doors for fear of the Jews, and this fear puts them on a level with others, earlier in the book, who did not confess their faith for fear of the Jews, and with Joseph of Arimathea, the secret disciple. The closed doors also confirm an aspect of the resurrection that has already been hinted at; John had mentioned the position of the napkin and the cloths in the tomb, perhaps to suggest that the body had been transformed into spirit and glory and passed through the material that had been wrapped around it. (Contrast Lazarus, who had to be untied.) Now, the risen Jesus (notice how John continues to use the personal name) comes in spite of the doors and stands among them. John uses the verb *come*, rather than *appear*, or *be seen*, just as he had done in the supper discourses (I will come again; I will come to you). He had promised them peace, and now he gives it to them. He identifies himself as the one who had been crucified. He had promised that they would rejoice, and now they do. He sends them, as he had been sent, again fulfilling the promises and predictions he had made at the supper. And he breathes on them, giving them the Holy Spirit, just as he had taught them to expect.

The saying that is unexpected is the final sentence, of forgiving and retaining sins. It is similar to a saying in Matthew, and it is probably a different version of it; but the problem is why John includes it here, since it is so out of character with the rest of his book. It is not out of character in Matthew's gospel, which includes provision for the church and officials with authority over others. John, we had thought, was not interested in the institutional aspect of the faith, and this is possibly the only place in the first twenty chapters where it appears. There are no other references to the forgiveness of sins in John, and it has been suggested that the saying was added by a redactor; but there is no manuscript evidence to support the hypothesis. A very inadequate explanation might be that authors sometimes made the end of their books come round to something that had been said at the beginning; in John, the Baptist had said at the beginning that the Lamb of God would take away the sin of the world; at the end, Jesus assures his disciples that this will be so, through their mission. Their testimony will bring release to those who believe, and condemnation to those who do not.

20.24–31 *The eighth day*

Where John's gospel ends, as in the case of Mark, presents us with a problem, but in this case it is more difficult to feel happy about any of the solutions that have been offered. In the case of Mark, there was the evidence of manuscripts, ancient translations and patristic quotations that the book ended with the fear and silence of the women; but all the authorities for the text of John include chapter 21, whereas the present paragraph looks as though it were meant to be the ending of the book.

It has therefore been suggested that chapter 21 was added later as an appendix, though not so much later that any copies of the gospel in its shorter form survived. This may be the best explanation of the awkwardness of the apparent double conclusion; but there is always the doubt about a hypothesis of this kind, that it rests on twentieth century feelings about first century practices. We cannot be sure that the author of chapters 1 to 20 may not have written and added chapter 21 himself. There is some evidence for a change of style and thought, but its value as an argument for change of author is disputed. The present position is the unsatisfactory one, that we cannot be sure why the gospel ends in this way.

We can, however, see that in this paragraph John has written a passage that could have formed the conclusion to his book; and we can see how he has done it and why it would have made a fitting ending, by working through it backwards.

He ends with a statement of his intention, which is also the key for the proper use of his gospel: he wants his readers (the word 'you' is plural) to have life. This is the eternal and abundant life, glory, salvation, freedom, and knowledge of the truth that has been the subject and theme of all that he has written. As he has told us again and again, this gift of God is a person, Jesus Christ, and not a thing or an idea, a law or a doctrine. Life cannot be received except by entertaining the one who gives life and remaining in a relationship with him which John refers to as believing. The purpose of the book that he is now bringing to its end is to make the continued availability of faith possible for his readers. Paul had said that faith comes from what is heard, that is, from the preaching of Christ; John is saying that faith comes from what is read, that is, from the written book. The book is like a sermon, and the author's aim is the same as the preacher's: that they may believe. Because John had this specific and limited aim, there was no need for him to included in his book more than a selection of the words and deeds of Jesus; John knows there were more things that Jesus did and said than he has written. It is possible that he is alluding to the other three gospels, or to some of them. He has, after all, recorded fewer miracles than any other evangelist, and some kinds of miracle are not included at all (exorcisms, and the cursing of the fig-tree). But he is confident that the book he has written and these selections that he has made for it of the words and deeds of Jesus are enough to provide material for the readers to have faith.

The readers, it is assumed, were not present at the time when the events took place; the book is a substitute for having been there at the time; that is, the book takes the place of seeing Jesus. But not to have seen is no disadvantage, because what matters is believing, not being present at a particular time or in a particular place.

The case of Thomas illustrates this: he was not there at the time when Jesus came to the disciples on the evening of the first day of the week, but he was told about it by the others; he had the possibility of believing through hearing, but he rejected it, and said that he would only believe if he had tangible proof. We have been prepared for this aspect of Thomas' character by the previous occasions on which he has spoken in the book: Let us go [into Judaea], that we may die with him . . . Lord, we do not know where you are going; how can we know the way? He represents unbelief and lack of understanding within the circle of the disciples. Though Jesus rebukes him for his faithlessness, he nevertheless provides precisely what Thomas had asked for, in exact detail: finger here, hand there.

Thomas is to believe, and all the readers of John's gospel can do what Thomas is commanded to do; Thomas has done it because he has seen; the readers will be more blessed than Thomas, because they will believe without seeing.

But though Thomas is rebuked, the final statement of faith is given to him; what he says goes beyond everything that has been said by any character earlier in the book, and brings us back to the prologue. Thomas says, My Lord and my God, reminding us that John had said at the beginning that the Word was God. Just as, as in the case of Peter, being the first of the disciples, the rock, and disowning Jesus three times, fit together appropriately in a faith that is more interested in grace than in success, so failing to believe and sticking out for proof go well with being chosen to have the final word that best expresses the truth, in a book that lays stress on the initiative and action of God.

21 *The appendix*

This final section of the book, in all the manuscripts and ancient translations that are available to us, forms one single continuous story: it begins with the setting out of disciples on a night fishing expedition and continues with the appearance of Jesus at dawn, the meal on the shore of the lake, the conversation between Jesus and Peter, and Peter's question about the disciple whom Jesus loved; this leads on to a further statement about the author and his book.

The scene is Galilee, and of the other gospels only Matthew records a resurrection appearance of Jesus there; the story of the catch of fish is similar to one in Luke, but there it comes at the beginning of the ministry. There are possible links with chapter 20: Peter and the disciple whom Jesus loved are mentioned together; the other disciple recognizes the truth before Peter, though Peter arrives before the others.

Failure to catch fish, followed by remarkable success, is generally taken as a sign pointing to the future ministry of the disciples; and this seems to have been Luke's understanding of it, too, and is seen in the command of Jesus there, Henceforth you will catch men. The number of fish caught has been discussed by commentators both ancient and modern, and various interpretations have been offered: that is to do with the different kinds of fish, or that it is a significant number, or that the number corresponds to the numerical value of Old Testament place-names. Of one thing we can be certain: John intends us to see that the catch was very large, and to note that the net was not torn. God can make disciples effective beyond their expectations, and can cope with the problems that such grace will produce.

The meal of bread and fish recalls that other meal in Galilee when the five thousand were fed, and the discourse that followed it. The disciples know that this is Jesus, the Lord, because of the continuity between what he did before his glorification and what he does after. He is still the one who provides the food, that is, he is the Saviour.

It has often been suggested that the conversation between Jesus and Peter that follows the meal is intended to be read as the re-instatement of Peter, and that the three questions of Jesus correspond to the three denials; that this is why Peter is grieved when Jesus asks the question for the third time. It may be so; certainly Mark had specifically referred to Peter in the message given to the women at the tomb, and that has been explained in the same way. According to the tradition quoted by Paul, Peter was the first to see Jesus after the resurrection, and in Luke there is also a reference to the appearance to Simon. Here we are told that Peter is to be the pastor of the Lord's flock, and, when he is old, to die as a witness to Jesus and to the glory of God; meanwhile, he is to follow Jesus as a disciple.

The command to Peter to follow joins this conversation to Peter's question: the disciple whom Jesus loved is following; what is to happen to him? Apparently there had been a belief in the community that the disciple would not die before Jesus came at the end of the age; but now he has died, and the end has not come. So the story is told to correct a mistake, and to show that Jesus did not say this: he told Peter to follow him, and that it was no concern of Peter's what happened to the other disciple.

There then follows the one place in the whole book in which it is explicitly stated that the disciple whom Jesus loved is the one who not only bore witness but also has written these things; and this is endorsed by an unspecified group: We know that his testimony is true. Some have taken this to mean that the author of the whole book is the disciple whom Jesus loved, and that that disciple is John the son of Zebedee, mentioned at the beginning of this chapter, but not elsewhere in this gospel. Others have read this passage as an example of pseudonymity, a device frequently used in the ancient world, by Jews, by Greeks and by Christians, to give force and authority to religious and other kinds of writing. How one reads the gospel will not depend on how one interprets this verse, but the interpretation of this verse will depend on an assessment of the gospel as a whole and of the relation between it and the other gospels.

Then, as in chapter 20, there is an explanation that the book includes only a selection of the deeds of Jesus, and the reason is given that the record of all he did would be more than the world could contain.

Retrospect

The title of this brief study of the gospel, *Finding the Way through John*, is deliberately and obviously ambiguous. As we come to the end of our reading of the text, it may help to put together an answer to the question, What is the way, according to John? What would his answer be, if we were able to interrogate him, and put to him this question: what is it you are really saying in your book?

He might begin by telling us that the fact that we are asking this question shows us something about ourselves: that we have not yet found what it is that he is offering us, through his book. We read his gospel and struggle to understand it, because we do not yet see the truth. This is his starting-point: he is writing a book that is meant to bring light to those who are in the dark, understanding to the ignorant; and to rescue those who are being destroyed.

Our problem, as John sees it, is that we do not want to acknowledge that this is our situation. We have come to terms with darkness, ignorance and mortality, and made a pact with death, so that we accept its limitations as the inevitable condition of life. We have learned to live with evil. To John this is a disastrous mistake that could cost us our lives.

John is one of those comparatively rare people who are dissatisfied with the way their contemporaries are living and horrified at the second-rate quality of what they find acceptable. He believes passionately that we could do better; and this dissatisfaction colours not only his view of those who are not believers, but also his attitude to the contemporary churches. Darkness and death are at work not only in the world, but among the faithful; it is because John is so much against what is going on in the churches at the time that he decides to write another gospel, to replace all previous gospels; by itself, he believes, it will be enough for faith and life and light.

The book he writes is full of stories of conflict between Jesus and the Jews, and this is one of the embarrassments that John presents to the contemporary reader. It is not just the unbelieving world that opposes Jesus, but even more those who have faith of a kind, and a religious system that enables them to cope with life as it is. Such people exist in any religious organization, and what John says about the Jews could equally well be said about the members of any religion, including Christians. John's anti-Jewishness is best understood as self-criticism.

To settle for the inferior is inevitably to reject the superior. Those who are in the dark gang up on the light and seem to succeed in putting it out. John writes with a new and different insight which, he believes, calls for the dismantling of what is going on, and a fresh beginning. Jesus, to John, is one who comes to us rejecting the past and saying that all who came before him were thieves and robbers; you must be born again; there can be no continuity with the past; its only function is to point to what is now appearing.

John applies this insight in particular to the way the Christians have turned Jesus into the founder of an institution, and developed customs and ways of thinking that make the group, the collective (as Matthew had), the starting point, rather than the individual. John does not speak about the church, or suggest that Jesus founded it; he scarcely refers to Christian initiation through baptism, or to the eucharist; he does not record teaching of Jesus on subjects that interest church people: nothing for example about bishops, presbyters and deacons, though these orders were almost certainly in existence at the time when he was writing. The only occasion when John uses the word apostle is to make the negative point: An apostle is not greater than the person who sent him.

John is able to jettison so much of the traditional religious baggage because he sees the way differently. As John presents him, Jesus did not come to offer a sacrifice for sin, or to make a new covenant, or to found a church, or to teach people how to keep the old law, or to give them a new law; he came to be himself. What he does, he does by being there; or rather, by being here, because John does not await a future coming. What makes the new way possible is the presence of the person who is both the Word through whom all things were made and Jesus who manifests himself to believers as their life and salvation. The meaning of the I AM sayings is that everything that is needed for the real and full life is Jesus, and is available through union with him.

It is because John sees it in this way that he must give priority to the individual over the institution, and to faith over any external and visible sign. There is no need for a sacred temple now, either in Jerusalem or in Samaria; there is no means of grace and no hope of glory, because grace is replaced by the indwelling Jesus, and hope is fulfilled already in his presence both with the Father and with the believer in a union that cannot be broken.

Just as John draws our attention away from the usual topics of theology – the atonement, eschatology, ecclesiology, ethics – so he also limits the way we think about the Spirit. The function of the Spirit is wholly to reveal Jesus, and to make it possible for us to know him and respond to him. There is no activity of the Spirit that is independent of Jesus; he does not teach new doctrines. The truth is Jesus, and the Spirit illuminates the mind to see him and know him, and to remain in him.

There is a new commandment, to love one another; and there is the prayer of Jesus, that the believers may be one; this is also what he means when he says, I thirst. The believers will come together in unity, as the rooms of a house make up one house, or as the branches of a vine are the vine. The unity, however, is personal, not that of an institution; John prefers the language of friendship and love to that of body and limbs, or stones and temple.

There is a final point which, if it were not made, would invalidate everything that has been said so far: though the message of John is Jesus, and though John's understanding of the way is that it consists of personal and individual union with him, there is more to be said than this. Jesus is nothing in himself, and can do nothing by himself. He is the Word of God, the Son of the Father, the agent, messenger and apostle of another. John's book is not Christo-centric, but theocentric. Union is with the one who laid down his life, and this is always how he is known and experienced: Jesus is at the disposal of his Father. To see him is to see the Father; and to know him is to know the Father. John agrees with the Jews: if Jesus had made himself equal with God, he would have been a blasphemer.

There can be no union with Jesus that is not union with God; and the union with God that is available through Jesus makes anything else seem wholly inferior, unnecessary and unsatisfying. It was this realization that made John so angry with the world, the Jews and the churches, and inspired him to write this extraordinary book.

Books on John's Gospel

The quantity of books on this gospel is such that anyone starting to study it may be dismayed. This note is meant to offer advice to beginners only; those who have read some of the literature will be able to judge for themselves.

First, there is a robust defence of an entirely different approach to this, in an essay by C. S. Lewis; the title of the essay is 'Fern-seed and Elephants' and it was published posthumously in a collection of his papers under the same title, *Fern-seed and Elephants* (Collins, Fount Paperbacks, 1975). A more recent book that also argues for this other way of reading John, but in much greater detail, is the late J. A. T. Robinson's *The Priority of John*, edited by J. F. Coakley (SCM Press 1985).

Those who want to study the text in English will find a great deal of help in the old *Revised Version of the Bible with marginal references* (Oxford 1898); these references help the reader to find the relevant Old Testament passages, and the parallel sections in the other three gospels.

Some people may want to read a Commentary on the gospel; and then the problem is, which to recommend when there are so many that are so good. Here is a list of half a dozen, arranged in the order in which they were published:

E. C. Hoskyns, edited by F. N. Davey, *The Fourth Gospel* (Faber 1940)

W. Temple, *Readings in St. John's Gospel* (Macmillan 1939 & 1942)

R. H. Lightfoot, edited by C. F. Evans, *St. John's Gospel* (Oxford 1956)

R. E. Brown, *The Gospel according to John* in The Anchor Bible (Doubleday 1966)

J. Marsh, *The Gospel of St. John* in The Pelican Gospel Commentaries (Penguin Books 1968)

B. Lindars, *The Gospel of John* in New Century Bible (Oliphants 1972)

For the reader with some knowledge of Greek there are also:
C. H. Dodd, *The Interpretation of the Fourth Gospel* (Cambridge 1953), especially Part III

C. K. Barrett, *The Gospel according to St John*, second edition (SPCK 1978)

But no list of books on John should be allowed to pass that does not include Rudolf Bultmann, *The Gospel of John*, (English translation, Blackwell 1971).

A short but difficult book that has considerably changed our understanding of John is E. Käsemann, *The Testament of Jesus*, (English translation, SCM Press 1968).

Finally, a small book that was published after this study had largely been written and that is strongly recommended is A. Ecclestone, *The Scaffolding of Spirit* (Darton, Longman & Todd 1987).